Making Hay while the sun shines

Making Hay while the sun shines

The life story of my journey to success.

By James Treanor

Bought in Glaslough, County Monaghan, on Saturday 5th April 2025 - on "Helens" Weekend Away

Dedicated to all wonderful, yet struggling minds, who desire a change in their lives. You can do it.

A Quote From Me to You...

Life is a journey from beginning to end, so remember my friend, as you walk through, that where you are now, so once was I, and as I am now, you will surely be, so do what you love and achieve your dreams, to have no regrets like me.

Contents

Introduction

I am just a man from humble beginnings, with huge dreams and high expectations. I love the things that most men do, like watching the football, having a game of pool, admiring fast cars, and putting an odd bet on a horse. I love the heat of the sun on a hot summer's day, but I love all the seasons, and the exceptional gifts that each of them brings. I admire the mystery of the moon and the stars in all their glory, and the mystery in the creation of our wonderful world.

I never warmed to the idea of spending by life working a 9 to 5 job and being told what to do and when to do it. I much preferred the idea of freedom, which is having both the time and the financial stability to live my life my way and do as I please. I started out with a job and ended up with an empire. I have written this book to tell you my story, and to inspire you to know that if I can do it, you can do it too. All you need is to commit to yourself, have a good attitude, and the desire to succeed. Just believe and know that you are enough and that you can achieve anything that you put your mind to.

My story is about the many challenges I faced, and how I grew from having nothing to having everything I wanted in life. I want to share my experiences with you in the hope that you will be inspired to take a leap of faith, whether it be in a new business, a change of career, or simply a change of lifestyle. You are never too old, and it is never too late. The past is gone, but you have today, which you should use to create tomorrow. You are unique in this world, created for a purpose. You have a talent and a skill that matches no other, so use these gifts to reach for the highest heights. I wish you endless blessings, success in all areas of your life, and happiness in abundance.

Chapter 1

The Younger Years

Infancy is not just for babies. Infancy is merely the beginning of anything new, whether it be a new life born into the world, or the beginning of a new experience or learning a new trade at any age. It is during this infancy stage that our minds are fed with the knowledge that create behaviours which become rooted in our subconscious mind. We practice these behaviours and they become natural to us as habits. And these habits are what determine how successful we are in every area of our lives. If a mother tells a child that he is amazing, he believes he is amazing and will grow up knowing that he is amazing. On the other hand, a child who is brought up in a negative environment, always being told 'No', and 'You can't do that', will grow up believing that they are limited in what they can do. The truth is that there are no limitations. You can do anything if you believe it.

It's like the story of the young boy who found a single egg lying in the farmyard and he put it in with the hens' eggs. The hen kept the egg warm with her own. When it was born, the baby bird was somewhat bigger and very different to the others. It was an eagle. However, the hen treated it just like her own, and her little chicks would all follow her around, pecking in the dirt and running around the farmyard. The young eagle often looked up into the sky at other birds flying along side the planes. He had big dreams and wished that he too could fly so high in the sky. This eagle didn't know he could do that. Because he was reared with chickens, he believed he was a chicken, and so he lived his life on the ground, pecking in the dirt, and never got to realize what he was truly capable of.

'What the mind of man can conceive and believe, he will achieve' Napoleon Hill.

I was blessed to come from a hardworking family, where farming was our way of life. I was the sixth child of seven children, born in 1943 when World War two had just come to an end. With so many Treanor's in the area, we all had nicknames to identify from which family we came, which were usually chosen according to our parents' names. So, because my father was called Peter, I was known as Jimmy Peter Treanor. Our family home stood in a 40-acre tillage farm in the rural area of Carrickroe in North County Monaghan. My father was quite the no nonsense man, an upstanding character, well thought of in our community, and his work ethic was one of great strength and consistence. Clocks and timetables were unheard of. He went to bed during the hours of darkness and worked during all the sunlight hours God supplied. Our farm yielded grains of corn, wheat and barley, and crops of numerous vegetables with potatoes being our largest crop. There was also the usual farm animals of cattle, hens, and pigs. All these commodities allowed us to be self-sufficient, or as they may call it now, living off the grid. It was truly a 'farm to table' process because we planted the corn, cut it, thrashed it, brought it to the mill to grind it, and then brought it home where it was used to make porridge for our breakfast, and as feed for the animals. Surplus harvest was sold, and sometimes brought to the market in Monaghan town. I used to be so excited when my father brought me to the trade market, which was 14 miles away. The journey took about 4 hours with the horse and cart, so we would leave very early in the morning, and arrive home late that night. The town would be buzzing with traders for horses, farm animals, food produce and fabrics.

My father was certainly one of the wealthier men of his time. When I say wealthy, I mean with assets, rather than material things. We were unspoiled, brought up without luxury or personal possessions. Clothes were handed down from sibling to sibling and nothing was wasted. And because we were brought up like this, we never acquired the desire to own material items or live in luxury. Any earnings were reinvested to accumulate more wealth. My father went on to buy more farms and he opened a shop to buy and sell local produce. He used to say that we should never confuse price with value and with this mindset he continued to invest wisely.

'The biggest risk of all is not taking one'
Napoleon Hill.

With no electricity, no running water, no tractors, and no employees, our farm was truly a family affair, and we each had an important role to play. Before going to school each morning, I walked to the well to bring home the water and fill up the barrels. The cows needed to be milked, and the eggs collected from the hens. On the way home from school, I gathered the potatoes and whatever vegetables were in season, for my mother to prepare for dinner for that evening. We spent many evenings gathering blackberries, that grew wild on the thorny bushes which lined the laneway. We collected the blackberries in baskets and brought them to the shop where they were weighed. It was competitive, each of us hoping that we would earn more than the other, according to the weight. The reward made the scratches and bleeding from the thorns pricking our fingers, worthwhile. My favourite time of year was the harvest season in August. It was the busiest time of the year when we spent all our time in the fields, including my mother, who used to lay a blanket on a soft bed of hay for the baby to sleep when all hands were needed. Cutting the wheat, making the hay, ploughing the fields, and planting new seeds, the work was endless. I remember my brothers and I prodding the stacks of corn with a pitchfork and the rats would jump out, sometimes even land on our chests. We were fearless and thrilled with the rush of adrenaline. Harvest time is one of my fondest memories as a child. It brought our family and the entire community together as we all came together and helped each other during this busy time. Although it was long hours of hard work, it was a joyous time of laughter and tremendous fun.

Emigration numbers were high at that time, mostly bound for England or the US. One day my uncle walked out of his home, and without telling anyone where he was going, he was never seen again. More recently, when looking into my family tree I discovered that he had won a travel ticket to get to the US on the Titanic. He survived the journey and raised a family in the US. If this happened today, I could imagine the ordeal with his picture on the Missing Persons List. But walking out and not coming back was quite common at the time.

My mother was a gentle, kind, and caring woman. Her homemade chicken soup was the cure to all illnesses. Her homemade breads and rabbit stews were made with love and kindness. I will never forget her oven bread. What we called an oven, was a large metal pot which hung on a crane crook over the open-hearth fire. She would mix currants through the dough and place it into the pot. With tongs, she would take some of the hot turf coals and place them on top of the lid of the oven. This created an even distribution of heat from the bottom to the top. This special method of baking produced an incredible flavour which simply cannot be repeated with today's conventional ovens. The currant bread was usually made on special occasions or when a visitor would come to the house. It would be carefully and evenly sliced and laid out on a fancy platter like a work of art.

I remember one visitor in particular. He was an elderly man who used to come visiting once a week. He would come in the late evening when it was dark. He came through the fields towards the back of the house, so nobody could see him coming. He would go straight to the henhouse and steel the eggs and hide them in the ditch of the laneway so he could take them on his way home after his visit. None of us noticed, until one evening my father was out in the bier when he saw the man coming out of the henhouse and hiding the eggs. He had caught him red-handed. His visits stopped for a while after that.

My mother churned her own butter using a staff which she pushed up and down in the barrel of milk. She skinned, and boned the chickens and rabbits, and with all that she had to do, I never heard her complain. I remember her as a happy person, always looking out for others, and praising every task we completed. I remember one evening when the wheel was broken on the horse cart, I worked on it for hours and even though I had probably made it worse, she said 'You are a great boy, you fixed the wheel, you can do anything'. This simple, yet positive reaction had a huge impact on my self-worth. I truly believed that I really could do anything. Henry Ford spent five years inventing the first car. He spent those five years finding out all the ways that wouldn't work and kept going until he found a way that it would work. Little did I realize at that time, that my mother was forming a positive mindset within me, building resilience and confidence that would stay with me forever. She was a devout Christian woman with strong faith. I remember her holding her rosary beads and bringing us together as a family to pray regularly.

My eldest sister, Mary Catherine reminded me of my mother in many ways. When I visited her home, she could never do enough to make me feel welcome and she was the same with everyone. She would show her love through food, always making tea, sandwiches, salads, and sweet treats. She was such a kind-hearted woman and a great mother.

'Write it on your heart, that every day is the best day of the year' Ralph Waldo Emerson

I remember when it was time for killing the pig, and my brothers and I would gather around watching. We were waiting to get the pig's bladder. After my father rinsed it in salt water, we would inflate it and tie a knot on the end of it. This was our football. We played a lot of football. We arranged a team and played against other teams from the parish. A very old bus would come and collect us and take us to different villages to compete. There was just about enough room for 12 of us, but there was just as much fun on that old bus, as there was at the game. We were very competitive and gave it our best. By half time we were exhausted and drank every drop of water from the small bottles we had taken with us. This gave me an idea. Before heading off to the next game, I filled as many bottles as I could find with fresh water from the well. I got some cola and put a few drops into every bottle to add sweetness and colour. This was my very first business idea. I carried the box of drinks onto the bus, and at the end of the game, I would sell them all for a penny each. The boys were so thirsty, they didn't question the cost. The addition of the cola made the water taste sweet, and my pocket was even sweeter. I made lots of pennies and the other teams bought from me too. I would gather the empty bottles, take them home, wash them and refill them, so I had even more for the next match.

At school I was more of a hinderance than a student. I was only there because I had to be, but I made the most of it by adding some humour. The only form of heating in the school was the huge fire which the Master lit every morning from the stack of sticks he kept in the entrance hall. One morning when he asked me to go to the hall and get more sticks for the fire, I headed off outside and didn't come back until it was home time. I pretended that I thought he meant the community hall a few miles down the road, instead of the entrance hall. Class numbers were large, as there were four year groups in one room. This made it difficult for the master to find out who had put the piece of whin bush on his chair which pierced his skin when he sat down, and who put the carbon powder into the fire to create the huge bang. We got the rod several times, but that was fine, because we knew it was coming and we were prepared. I had a horse's hair in my pocket. I would take the horses' hair, loop it around my thumb and small finger so it stretched tightly across my palm. Each time the rod came down, it would bounce off the hair. We had to pretend that it hurt, so we forced a few tears and held our breath to make our faces turn red. Teachers at that time used their own discretion to punish anyone who stepped out of line. A lot of us suffered severe whacks on our hands and legs with his cane, so some days on my way to school when I saw one of the neighbours ploughing his field, I would jump on the cart beside him and spend the day working instead.

Aunt Susan, my father's aunt, who lived with us would call into the school for a visit and ask, 'Who has the currant bread for lunch today?' Only the posh kids would have it for a school lunch and the others would have the more common simple soda bread. Being a neighbourly woman and wanting to know everything about everyone else, she enjoyed visiting the school and the neighbours to keep up with all the gossip. As a boy, I thought that Aunt Susan was an old lady. I guess when we are just a kid, we think that anyone over the age of forty is ancient. But Aunt Susan was far from old. Her own father had lived through and survived the Famine, so she had lots of stories to tell. Aunt Susan had a vegetable patch outside our home which she cherished, and I remember her eating raw bean shoots and pea shoots from her garden every day. She grew herbs and plants and had lots of tips and tricks to keep the insects away. Because of her background and upbringing through pro famine Ireland, this was the way of life. She was physically as fit as an athlete, even at 95 years old. There is a lot to be said for being self-sufficient and consuming fresh wholesome produce. There was no choice at that time, but her healthy eating habits certainly gave her health and longevity. She was a smart tough, hardworking lady, who left it difficult for us to outwit her.

It wasn't all work and no play. We had a great social life. Dances every weekend in the local hall, playing cards with the neighbours, house parties, and community events. I learned to play the accordion and joined the local band. We made our own fun too, as well as a few bottles of poitin. At night when walking home, a few of us would stop along the road and under the light of a candle we would play a game called pitching pennies. We told lots of ghost stories and chased foxes with pellet guns. One evening a few of us planned to play a prank an old widow, after a rumour of ghost stories going around the week before. The woman lived with her son and always went out to the bier to milk her two cows every evening at the same time, so this made our planning easy. I took one of my mother's syrup cans, and filled it with carbon powder, which was used to light the lamps. When I met up with the boys, we bored a hole in the top of the tin with a nail. About an hour before milking time, we headed down to the bier and set it up. We spat on the carbon which made it sizzle, secured the lid, and then put the can carefully in the corner of the bier. We had dipped the string in paraffin oil and cut it long enough for us to put one end through the nail hole and hold the other end as we hid behind a bush outside. Sure enough, the old widow came out at the predicted time, settled the two cows into place, sat on her old wooden stool, and started milking into the tin buckets. We waited with excitement until she had the buckets half full. Then we lit the string. We watched as the flame quickly headed down the line and finally reached the can. The explosion was immense. The widow jumped about 6ft high off the stool, and the cows knocked over the buckets of milk. She came running out of the bier screaming and shouting. We ran so fast down the field, tripping over each other with laughter.

On a winters evening, just as it was beginning to freeze, we would wheel a barrel of water down to the road near the school. The road was long with brays, dips, and bumps, which were perfect for our slide. We emptied the barrel onto the road and watched the water running down the hill and over the bray. By nightfall, the ice had formed. We slid from the top to the bottom, jumping into the air on every dip. Sometimes we would end up in the hedge and our skin was covered in blisters from the nettle stings and scrapes from the thorn bushes. I remember a time when we all got into the empty barrel, which sat on a crate with wheels. It was jam packed with as many of us as possible, all squeezing in for the thrill. There were legs and arms hanging out from all sides. When the wheels were set in motion, the boys on the side-line shouted and cheered with laughter as they watched us in the barrel speeding down the hill. In one of my turns my leg was hanging off, scraping along the gravelled road, but nobody heard my shouting above the laughter and cheers. The blood poured from my knee to my ankle as the skin was grazed and ripped. We laughed even more and still did it all over again the following day.

I finished primary school at 12, and like many others at that time, I didn't move on to secondary school. I was excited, and with so many goals, I couldn't wait to begin my journey in the real world. My first goal was to buy a bicycle. I was delighted when I heard of a farm in Northern Ireland looking for workers to gather potatoes in the fields for five shillings a day. This was something in which I had great experience, so I decided to go. One of my close friends at that time also wanted a bicycle, and I couldn't wait to tell him about the opportunity, and he too could buy a new bicycle. However, when he said he wasn't prepared to go such a journey and to gather potatoes all day, I was shocked. I couldn't believe that this boy who said he wanted a bicycle so much, wasn't prepared to do the work to achieve it. It reminded me of the story of the wise old man who was known as the richest man around at that time. He was sitting at the edge of the lake when he was approached by a young boy asking him how to be rich and successful. The old man asked the boy if he was sure that he really wanted to know. The boy said 'yes, I really want to know', so the wise old man grabbed the boys head and held it under the water in the lake. The boy was unable to breath and fighting for his life. When the old man eventually let his head up, the boy shouted, 'why did you do that?' The old man said, how badly did you want to breath? 'When you want success and money as bad as you wanted that last breath, you will be rich and successful'. This story lived with me....

'Always focus on the reward because the work to achieve it is the only route'

I went ahead on my own to Northern Ireland and after 3 summers of gathering potatoes for 5 shillings a day, I bought my new bicycle for fifteen pounds. The long days spent with tired legs, scratched hands and sacrifice had paid off. It was a dream come true. I rode my new bicycle everywhere and cared for it as if it were the only one in the whole world. I was always fixing it up, washing it, adding to it and making it more than just a bicycle. I knew my bicycle inside out, every nut and bolt, every spoke and thread, and I was very interested in the mechanics of how it all worked. Neighbours would call with their broken bicycles and ask me to fix them, and I became known as the local mechanic. Before that, I was known as the community hairdresser, as many came to me to get their hair cut. However, I preferred being known as the local mechanic. My interest led to me taking up a position as an apprentice mechanic in Clerkin's garage in Monaghan town. I rode 14 miles every morning to work for 22 shillings a week. There were very few cars around at that time, so any cars that did come in was a whole new learning experience for me. I quickly learned a lot and developed a huge interest in mechanics and machinery. Maybe that's why I stayed for so long because it certainly wasn't for the money. After paying 17 shillings a week for lunch out of 22 shillings, I was left with only 5 shillings on a Friday evening. You see, I had another goal – I wanted to buy a car and if I stayed here, I wasn't going to achieve that.

‘Give a child a car, and it will become a piece of scrap in 2 years. Make a child work for a scrappy car and it will become a car in 2 years.

Chapter 2

A New Adventure

At that time, two of my older brothers Louis and Michael, had emigrated to England to work. They told me how great it was there, and about the many opportunities there was to earn good money. In 1960 when they came home for my sister Mary- Catherine's wedding, I decided I wanted to go back to England with them with the goal of becoming rich. So, at 16 years old, in 1960, I travelled across the English Channel on a boat with my two brothers. They got me a job right away on the same building site as themselves in Luton for 12 pounds a week. I was ecstatic. What a difference in 12 pounds and 22 shillings. Every Friday when I got my paycheque, the first thing I did was send money home to my mother. I was so happy to be able to do this. She had given her life to us, and I wanted to share my earnings with her. I have always believed that when our parents get older, it is our turn to look after them, as they did for us. I excelled in Luton, and stayed there for about a year, where I quickly learned to drive diggers, lorries, and dozers. With my interest in mechanics and eagerness to operate them, nothing would stop me from excelling, so I thrived in the work. I lined and built foundations and excelled in all areas of the building trade. I was a likeable lad with a great sense of humour and built lots of friendships everywhere I went. I was also a 'Yes Man', so whenever anyone needed anything, I was always willing to help. One morning the site manager asked me to collect his wife every morning at 10m to work the canteen and leave her home again at 4 in the evening. The perk for this was that I could start and finish my work at the same times, for the same pay. Of course, I said yes. I hurried and got my driver's license and bought myself a Ford 10 van. I quickly learned to navigate the streets of Luton. For an Irish country boy, this seemed like a daunting task, but I saw it as an opportunity rather than a difficulty. I never thought for a moment that I didn't know the streets or may even get lost on the way. In every task, whether driving a digger for the first time, building foundations from scratch, or navigating city streets, I saw accomplishment, I saw opportunity and I just did it! I was fearless and everything was possible.

Most of the world's great inventions have been accomplished by people who persisted in trying even when there seemed to be no hope. We don't realize what we're capable of until we try something new. The only thing stopping you is your thoughts. Think big and trust in yourself with no doubts in your mind. Taking risks leads to a road of opportunities which will only be seen when you learn and grow along the way. Leonardo Da Vinci realized his potential when he was mentored by his father as an artist. When he left his home in Florence to open his own workshop in Milan, he wasn't earning enough money to survive, so he began looking for employment. He wrote letters to the king, claiming that he had studied weapons of war and knew of ways to improve them which would strengthen the King's position against his enemy. This was a bold move of confidence, but he was reaching high, seeking employment from the richest, yet most dangerous and powerful employers of his time. His words left no choice for the King, but to hire him, and Leonardo could set a high price. He used his employment opportunities, through difficult war times, to excel in engineering and the creation of new weapons through his drawing. Some of them worked and some of them didn't. But he never gave up trying. He created drawings of the Ariel Screw, which led to the invention of the first helicopter.

I have huge admiration for great inventors. The one trait they have in common is persistence. They have huge dreams and expectations and spend many years working to fulfil them. Fear of failure is not an option. When you s something new, it could take ten years b you reach the year that will change your life.

'The fear of failure is the greatest stumbling block to success'

'The greatest fear is fear itself' Franklin D. Roosevelt.

I left Luton to work on a block of flats in Oxford Street in London. When I arrived in London, I was hit with the need for a little more education than I had, which was very little. The underground with all its colour coded lines and different station names was a minefield. It was essential for me to navigate them and gain the knowledge I needed to survive here. These trains waited for nobody. If I wasn't at the right stop at the right time, I would be lost for hours. I think this was the first time in my life that I began to study. I studied the chart and learned fast. One morning on the site, I watched as one of the new workmen arrived an hour late to work. The poor man couldn't quite get his head around the train lines. The manager sent him home and told him to start work the following Monday when he could learn to be on time. This was a huge lesson for us all. This man, with a much higher level of education than me, didn't think he could learn any more. He had a college degree but couldn't read the train schedule. This is when I realized that the college of life is my favourite college. In this college, I can learn all the important things to be successful in life. In his college he only learned the subject of history. When he got his certificate, he was finished learning because he had achieved his desired level of education with honours. While he sat in his college learning about the past, I was working and earning in my college of life. I knew how to survive.

My college is living and learning every single day. There is no certificate to say that I am finished learning, because I will be always learning until the day I die. Don't get me wrong here, education is great, if you use it with a purpose. I believe that the greatest education is self-taught through practical experience in your chosen field. If you want to be a salesman, get a job sweeping the floors in the salesman's office, and listen to how he does it. If you want to be a writer, buy the books from the most successful writers, and read them. Associate with the people who have become successful in the same field. Never take advice from those who are not in the field themselves, or those who have failed. Surround yourself with likeminded people. The greatest secret to a happy life is to do something you love and find a way to make money at it. This way your work will be your hobby, so it is not work anymore. You will be excited to get out of bed every morning and look forward to the day ahead. I know so many people who are unhappy because they hate their job, but they will stay in their job until they retire at 65. They are working to earn a living, instead of earning a living while enjoying life to the full.

'You will become like those with whom you associate'

'Live your life to your full potential and enjoy each and every day'

After about a year in London, a huge snowstorm hit in 1962. It continued to snow for weeks, until it was so deep that all the building work had to stop. London came to a standstill and a lot of the men returned home because they had no work and no money. Two of my friends Paddy Slater, originally from Sligo, and Bob, from London, suggested that we go to Guernsey, where the weather was great, and work was plentiful. We left London and headed to the port where we took a ferry to Guernsey. It was a beautiful seaside resort where cafes and shops lined the streets. It is famous for its beaches and is known for having one of the world's largest tidal ranges, transforming the coastline every six hours. The island was once connected to France, until rising sea levels separated it from the mainland. We got jobs working in the fields, gathering potatoes. When the potatoes were bagged and ready for export, we loaded the lorry up and headed to the port to load them onto the boat. On the way, and while the lorry was in traffic, we would take turns to jump off the lorry to grab sandwiches and snacks off outdoor tables and quickly hop back on the lorry as it moved off. Some of the diners would run after the lorry, but thankfully we never got caught. With no accommodation, we slept under ferns in the fields and spent our days gathering potatoes to get a paycheque at the end of the week. It was such an adventure. We spent the weekends in the local pub, made so many friends, and enjoyed every moment. I was glad I didn't join the many others who had headed home because of the snow. We took an adverse situation and turned it into an opportunity for a whole new adventure.

'A positive mind will see opportunities instead of obstacles'   Brian Ford.

When the winter was over, and the snow had cleared in London, we headed back to re-join the building trade. When I discovered that my brother Louis had moved on to Kings Heath in Birmingham, I went there to join him. I started working on the same building site as Louis and met many more Irish people. There were so many of us, we started an Irish Association, of which I was elected the head leader. We would meet up to socialize in a hall, called the Irish Centre every weekend and our group grew bigger and better every week. We would welcome new immigrants and arrange jobs and accommodation for them. The work was so plentiful here in Birmingham, it was here that I earned not just plenty of money, but a solid reputation. My wages increased, my reputation increased, and I started to make some real money. At this point, with my growing confidence, I wanted more. I bought my first digger at 19. I continued to work on the building sites, and at 5 o'clock when all the workers went home, or to the local pub, I started working my second job, which was contracts I had secured form local authorities to line out and construct foundations for houses, flats, and commercial buildings. I worked all the hours God sent, ceasing every opportunity which presented itself. Time didn't matter to me. I wasn't one of the guys who downed tools at 5 o clock, just because it was 5 o clock. I saw finishing time as an opportunity for me to grow my own success. I continued to invest in more plant and machinery and created employment opportunities for many. I remember wheeling full barrows of concrete up narrow planks, climbing several stories high, for several hours at a time. It was like a powerful full body workout without the need for a gym. We were natural body builders with bulging muscles and great strength. We were physically fit, and no task was ever too much.

'We all have 24 hours in the day, you can spend them dreaming of your goals, or taking action to make them happen'. How you spend them is up to you'

One of the site managers asked me to go to Nottingham to finish the building of five houses and after being offered an irresistible paycheck, I bought myself an Austin Cambridge car and drove to Nottingham. I was excited for the opportunity to see the city, home to the famous Robin Hood and his merry men. I had heard the stories of Robin Hood, one of the world's best loved folk heroes who stole from the rich to give to the poor. I didn't get to walk through the majestic Sherwood Forest, which was once a huge royal hunting ground. I completed the building project successfully and headed back to Birmingham. I continued to work in Birmingham and eventually bought a Jaguar car. I remember walking into the garage and buying the car outright with cash. When I drove it down to the Irish pub, and took the boys for a spin, a lot of heads turned in admiration and I felt like a king. I was on top of the world. You see, all my work paid off. I was living my dream life. I had earned it. I had my dream car. When I look back, I realize that the best part of the car was the journey to achieving it. Now that I had it, I enjoyed it, but then I set yet another goal. I often hear people saying, 'if only I had a car, I would be made up', or 'if only I had a house, I would be happy', or 'if only I could go on a holiday, I would be happy'. You see, life is a journey and there is no destination. Most people think that there is an Ivory Tower. When they get the car, they thought would change their life, it gives them temporary happiness, and when this happiness dwindles, they become disappointed. Happiness is not in material things. Happiness is within you, no matter where you are or what you have. People say that far away fields are greener, but the truth is that they are green everywhere. You just need to open your eyes and your mind to see it. Happiness is deep within yourself and is created through the gratitude of everything you have. I remember a friend of mine who booked a holiday 3 months in advance. He spent every day of those 3 months thinking only about his holiday, and nothing else mattered. However, for those 3 months, it seemed like he had cancelled his life. He couldn't wait for the days to pass. He forgot to enjoy each day of those 3 months. It is good to look forward to something, but never lose the enjoyment of every day on the journey to each goal.

'Life is a journey and there is no destination'
Ralph Waldo Emerson.

Ambitions, goals, and achievements are the means to success. But no matter how small or big your achievements are, they keep you moving, learning, and fruitful. Working towards something keeps us alive and gives us a reason to keep going, but the most rewarding part is the journey on the way. It will bring many challenges, which help us to grow. There will be struggle and obstacles but solving them makes us stronger and more resilient. We learn through experience. In all cases determination will see us through. I remember one night in Birmingham when I had a job to finish by the next morning, my digger broke down. It was 11 o clock at night, with no garages open to get the parts I needed to fix it. The only thing on my mind was that I needed to get this job done somehow, and I couldn't let a broken digger stop me. I stood looking into the engine and all its mass of wires and terminals. After much thought, I disconnected the broken lead and continued to work without it. Even though it was a huge imposition, and what took 6 hours to complete instead of 3, I got the job done with the use of only 2 levers instead of three and had the job done just before the block layers arrived at 8am. You see, I focused on the goal, and rose above the obstacles. It would have been easy to drop the job and say, 'I can't do it because my digger broke down', but I wasn't a quitter, and when I said I was going to do something, I did it. The 'How' is just a matter of mindset, and mine was unwilling to let anything beat me. Not everything can be fixed. This goes for people as well as things. There is a difference in not giving up on something, and letting it go. Some things are out of our control, and some people will never change, no matter how hard we try. It takes wisdom to know the difference and courage to accept it and move on.

'The greater the obstacle, the stronger the man' Julias Ceaser

Now I want to point out that my intention is not boastfulness. In fact, my brothers Louis and Michael also excelled, and their success and financial worth greatly exceeded mine. Between them both, they built empires which yielded jobs for hundreds of employees, and I greatly admired them both. You see success is not just about money and wealth. Success is reaching your goals, no matter how small or big. My sister Margaret, who joined the nuns and trained as a nurse, became highly successful in her work. After leaving the convent, she went on to become head matron of a ward in a hospital in London. She became a midwife and climbed to the top of the ladder in the nursing profession. She then became sole carer of the Prime Minister's father. Margaret was the most caring person I ever knew. With her earnings, she fed the poor, gave to the homeless and walked around the streets of London, helping all those in need, by giving all she had.

Success didn't change me. I was still one of the lads. I didn't buy lavish clothes or let my wealth change who I was. I came from humble beginnings, and never forgot that. I continued to socialize and enjoy the simple pleasure of life, just the same as I did when I was a young lad earning five schillings a day. The only difference now was that I had the means to help others. I was happy to be the one to give somebody a lift home, or the lend of a car. Only those with much can give much. The best part of having plenty was the ability to give plenty to those in trouble or those in need. Giving is much more joyful than receiving when it is given with heart and willingness. In saying that, I was not an easy target for handouts. There are many able men out there who are just lazy and think that the rest of us should pay their way, while they sit back and do nothing. I believe that this kind should not be helped or given food. There are many who squander their earnings on their addictions and hobbies and expect others to bail them out. Yes, we all get into difficulties, and some through no fault of our own and we need help to get out of unexpected situations, and these are exceptions, but we cannot help anyone who is not prepared to help themselves. I remember helping a man out who was left homeless because of his alcohol and gambling habits. I gave him a house to live, rent free until he could afford the payments. I gave him a job to work, with opportunities to grow. However, he continued his old habits and took advantage of the help I had provided. He never showed up to work on a Monday, because he was suffering from the ill effects of the weekend. I realized that because I had helped him in the way I did, he didn't need to help himself. I had given him the necessary means to live so he didn't have to change his ways. Perhaps I served him an injustice by helping him too much. He left his job and took advantage of others and the last

I heard of him, he had lost his family and his friends. We must differentiate between those in need and those taking advantage. We can add fuel to the fire of an addict. We can add fuel to the fire of laziness and deceit. This is not help, this is deepening the hole in which they are stuck. If you see someone in a pit, don't dig them out. Offer them a shovel to dig themselves out instead. Only then they will grow, mature, and become independent. They will also be less likely to fall back into the pit a second time.

In another instance, I was about to proceed down a set of steps from the post office which was next to a supermarket. There was an elderly lady standing at the top of the steps with shopping bags by her side. When she said hello to everyone who passed her by, I knew that she was trying to get someone's attention. I stopped and asked her if she was alright. She told me that she had been standing there for thirty minutes, hoping that someone would help her to carry her bags down the steps. Her husband had been taken to hospital with a heart attack the night before. He had usually made the shopping trip with her, but this time she was alone, and with a recovering hip replacement, she was afraid that she wouldn't make it down the steps without falling. I carried the lady's bags to her car, and she continued on her way. We never know another person's circumstances. We should be more aware of the people around us and always offer a helping hand to those in need. Charity is not just about giving money. It is about giving a helping hand and thinking of others. It's about spending a few moments of your time to listen to someone. I guess there were over thirty people who had passed by that lady on the steps that morning. They were all too busy consumed in their own world, oblivious to those around them. They forget that they too will be elderly someday and may also need the assistance of a kind-hearted person along the way. Sometimes we avoid our neighbour because we don't feel like saying hello. I have been in shops where someone I know will hide behind a stacked shelf, rather than take a few moments to greet an acquaintance. I have witnessed queues at the airport security gates where people skip the queues and claim that they are in a hurry and don't want to miss their flight. They think that they are more important than everyone else there, even though they too are in the same queue with the same purpose.

I continued my building trade and was awarded several other contracts but always returned to Birmingham to be with my family and friends. I remember one Irish girl who got a job as a bus conductor. We would see her often as she would shout a big 'Yo Ho' across the street from the door of the bus. In a huge city, among hundreds of thousands, she could always see us from a distance. There was never a dull moment, and the craic was great. There were others who would mutter a hello under their breath and have a weary look of gloom on their face. When I asked them how they were today, they would spurt a list of complaints about the bad weather, the low wages, the polluted city streets, and the price of food. I hadn't noticed any of these things and couldn't understand why they thought like this. I thought the weather was great every day, the opportunities were plentiful, the city streets were buzzing, and the food was fabulous. Maybe he was spoiled as a child and needed to spend a while in the Sahara Desert, or in a famine ridden city where the hot sand blows into his eyes all day and the drinking water is brown. Or perhaps his legs should be temporarily amputated, or his eyesight diminished for a time. Maybe then he would see what he truly had and be grateful for it. I decided to avoid these kinds of people and avoid the negative vibes from them. I believe that no matter what this man had or where he was, he would always find something to complain about. What a sad way to live, to miss out on the joys of life. I was young, fearless, and enjoying life. I had accumulated many assets and developed my entrepreneurial talents, as well as forming skills and trades which would ordinarily take a lifetime to achieve. A positive mindset was obviously a huge part of my happiness.

'My greatest asset in life is myself'

In 1965 England was preparing to bring in the North Sea Gas through the Easington Terminal. It was a huge operation, and I was asked to carry out the work in burning out the existing pipes, digging down to the mains and fitting new pipes for the new gas to be installed in their place. It was a well-paid opportunity, so I spent one year in Kent, successfully fulfilling the contract. It was a difficult undertaking with great responsibility as we had to manoeuvre the plant and machinery on busy streets, while following the strict regulations to complete the project. It was a highly skilful process as the boring and depth had to be precise. A lot of work was done in the evenings, when the traffic and pedestrians were at their lowest levels. Kent was a beautiful place, with magnificent beaches and amazing scenery. It was one of the richer places of England and it wasn't hard to see why. It was a short journey from London, so tourists flocked to the area to enjoy holidays and day trips to the beach. Being in the south of England, closer to France, the weather was warmer, and the evenings were brighter. There was an array of restaurants, cafes, and shops and the nightlife was buzzing. We made many memories and met some great friends. I didn't know at that time, that this would be my last job before returning home to Ireland in 1969.

Chapter 3

Everything starts with an idea

I left my brothers and my life in England and came home to Ireland to fulfil a contract to build a golf course in a small village outside Monaghan called Glaslough. I purchased the necessary plant and machinery, gathered the necessary workers, and prepared to begin the new project. When I was told that the necessary paperwork wasn't quite in order, and the owner had some further red tape to cut through, I sought out other opportunities while they sorted out their difficulties. The local authorities were busy developing the town and constructing new roads at that time. I hired my plant to them to build bridges, so that my assets continued to work for me. An asset should never be left idle. It must be productive and lucrative to keep financially stable. My first find was a large 3-acre field at Cornacassa, which stood on the edge of Monaghan town. I walked through the field with a vision. It was the perfect location for a small housing development. I could always imagine the finished project – how it will look, and where and how it should be developed. By walking through the field, I was planning the number of houses, the location of the utilities and the connections. I was lining out the foundations in my mind. I knew that it would work so I didn't hesitate any further, and I purchased the field. I employed an architect to seek planning permission to build five houses, which didn't take long to acquire at that time and with still no green light on the golf course project, I began the new development. They were fine single story detached houses, which I designed and built to a very high standard. There was a great demand for the properties, and each one sold before the next one had begun. The pace of sales kept the work moving fast and financially viable. Twelve months past, and the golf course project fell through. I guess the red tape was much more than the owner could detangle. However, I wasn't disappointed. I never waited for anyone. It was never in my character to depend on someone else. Had I waited for the golf course project to begin, I would still be waiting today. Life does not always turn out the way you plan and expect it to. Many ideas and plans fall through for many reasons. In this case maybe the owner had not realized that the obstacles were too great to overcome, or perhaps the red tape was just too much. When we begin a new project, the first step is to plan. The first thing is to always know the rules and regulations and when these are confidently met, the obstacles will be eliminated. After that, there are only challenges, which are fun and easily overcome through experience.

If you fail to plan, you plan to fail' Benjamin Franklin.

Never waste your time, waiting on someone else to be successful, so that you too can be successful. We all make our own success. I could have sat and waited and blamed the golf course owner for my failure. I could have said that he made me come back to Ireland, and he made me invest in the plant and machinery which is wasted now. I could have become disheartened, angry, and maybe even depressed. You see, when I was told that the paperwork for the golf course wasn't ready, I said, 'ok, you can call me when it is' and I walked away. At that moment, it was up to me to either wait or to seek other opportunities while waiting. It is so easy to blame others for our own failures and adversities. I wait for nobody. My success is my choice. My failure is a result of my choices. Every decision we make today, is a steppingstone to where we will be tomorrow. I am responsible for myself, and I am in charge of my own destiny.

'If it is to be it is up to me' William Johnsen.

I completed the housing development and got married and started a family in 1970. I bought more land and built more houses. We made our home in one of 2 houses which I built at Drumhirk, an area about a mile out of Monaghan town. There was a piece of land alongside the 2 houses, which was swampy and continually flooded. The local farmers had labelled it as wasteland, unfit for any purpose, but I liked the land and its location. A tributary of the Blackwater River ran down along the side of the property, and I could see its beauty.
It was large enough to build a family home and with almost 2 acres, it also had the space and potential to be developed further. After walking through the field and weighing up all the pros and cons, I bought it. I brought in all my machinery and drained the field. I laid pipes and drains and turned the swampy wasteland into a beautiful family home. I laid lawns and footpaths, and built a large, detached

garage at the back. The house was very fine with a balcony to the front and arches which surrounded the front door entrance. Every one of the houses I had built, were built to a very high standard, double insulated and finished with fine detail to make them aesthetically appealing and different from others, but our new family home exceeded them all.

At that time, fireplaces were a difficult item to source for a new home. The nearest supplier was in Dundalk, a town about 30 miles away. Many home buyers asked me to source a fireplace for them, as they didn't wish to travel so far, and they also trusted my judgement to choose on their behalf. I drove to Dundalk to see the fireplaces, and watched how they were made, which sparked a new idea in my mind.

'Everything starts with a thought or an idea'

I set up a small workshop in the garage behind our home and started to make some fireplaces. I was amazed at the demand, and soon became overwhelmed with the number of customers I had wanting me to make one for them. With my building work still underway, and now the demand for fireplaces increasing, there just wasn't enough hours in the day for me. I spent days on my knees, levelling concrete floors and came home in the evening to start making fireplaces. One evening after finishing a floor in time for the plasterer to proceed with his part, my knees were crippled with pain. The cold wet concrete had taken its toll, and my knees were stripped of skin, leaving the raw flesh visible. I slept with a stool in my bed so that the blanket wouldn't touch my knees. I wrapped them with a dressing and continued to work all the hours that God supplied. With only a few hours sleep at night, and sometimes no sleep at all, I knew that I had to increase my production rate, or my health would continue to suffer. I began with building a new shed. It was a huge shed with a large workspace, storage loft, and staff facilities. I bought saws, polishers and equipment and created the first fireplace manufacturing plant in Co, Monaghan. Being the determined character that I am, I had to be sure of consistency and avoid a total dependency of walk-in customers,

I approached the local authorities and secured a contract to supply and install all the fireplaces they would need for social housing. I employed and trained men to make fireplaces, while I went out to install them. I travelled to Dublin regularly to buy raw materials of marble and granite. I further developed the site and built a new showroom and offices and my employee numbers increased.

A lot of us think that when we have more money we will have less problems, but I discovered that quite the opposite is true. The bigger the business, the more challenges and issues will arise. The more employees and customers I had, the more responsibilities I had. I watched small businesses with only two or three employees, who were successful and made a good living. They had less money, but also had a lot less difficulties and challenges to face. They worked at their own pace, whereas I worked towards deadlines and managed multiple tasks at once. On the other hand, because their workload was less, their rewards were less. There is nothing wrong with that. We will reap the rewards of what we sow.

Soon, customers came from all over the country wanting to buy my fireplaces. I created new designs, and my building experience allowed me to solve customer problems of smoke related issues with chimneys, chimney sizes, and sorts of challenges that came with the trade. By word of mouth, I gained a reputation of being the best and most reliable supplier within my competition. I always had to be the best and have the biggest range of choice. I went as far as creating a breath-taking masterpiece and placed it as the first showpiece visible on entering the showroom. I would watch the customers jaw dropping mmoment as they admired the beauty of the tall Portuguese marble fireplace, fit for a palace. I didn't expect to sell it and put a very large price tag on the mantle. I wanted it to stand as a mere symbol that they were in the best showroom in Ireland, but you wouldn't believe how many of those masterpieces I sold. I remember my yard being filled with so many customer cars, that they had to park along the roadside and walk about 500 yards to get to our showroom. I would be in the showroom all day and sometimes up until midnight, without getting ten minutes to have something to eat. I always stayed open in the late evenings and at weekends, as this was the time that couples could come to choose their fireplaces, outside of their own working hours. It certainly helped that I had the 'gift of the gab'. I was a people person, and always managed to seal the deal. In many cases, I had to call to the customers home to take correct measurements and make each fireplace to suit their specifications. In any case, I always related to my customers. Perhaps this is the greatest key to my success in sales.

When I drove up to a customer's house, I checked out my surroundings. I figured out before I got out of the car if I should put on my tie, or my blazer, or if I should just go as I was in my usual pair of chinos and shirt. I kept a pair of highly polished black shoes in my boot, beside a box of fancy home magazines and brochures. So, if it was a busy farmhouse, I approached as a farmer. I could relate to the customer and chat about the farm and all its greatness. If it was the home of a houseproud lady, with newly fitted carpets, I would put on my dust free blazer, change into my highly polished shoes, and offer to remove them at her front door. If I entered a house with which the walls were decorated with paintings of horses, I would admire them and begin by chatting about horses. I respected my customers and their environment. It was their home and their space, into which I was being invited and I needed to gain their approval before they would spend their money with me. Each customer mattered to me because for every job I successfully completed, another one stood to be gained. These people would tell their neighbours, and their family and friends. In the showroom I made a point of asking my customers how they came to know about me, and in almost all cases, they were told that I had done a fabulous job for one of their friends. I learned that few customers come in, see something they like and just buy it.

People buy from people. Business is all about people first and the product second. Respect, consideration, understanding, and patience are gained first. Then the selling of the product comes easily.

I met with many kinds of people over the years. Some had encountered very sad and difficult times and I sympathized with them. I remember one lady in particular whose eighteen-year-old daughter had gone to Spain on holiday and never came home. She had gone on holiday with her friends and went missing on a night out. The lady travelled to Spain and with the help of the police did everything possible to find her daughter, but there was no trace of her. Five years later, she is still looking for her child.

I remember sitting in a farmer's house, who wanted to cancel his order for a new fireplace. He told me that his 100 head of cattle had just been slaughtered the day before, due to an outbreak of TB. His livelihood had been shattered overnight, and he didn't have the finance to start again. I became sympathetic towards the man, who had a family of eight, all depending on only him. After walking around his farm with him, I listened to his success stories and how he came to owning this many cattle to begin with. He was a hard-working dedicated man and this tragedy had come to his door through no fault of his own. We sat down together and worked out a plan which I backed financially. I invested in the man because he was investable. He had the determination and mindset needed to succeed, and he did.

'Never be afraid to ask for help – Investors are ready and willing to back investable people'

I called to the homes of millionaires, castle owners, celebrities, and famous singers. I treated every one of them with the same respect I gave to those on social welfare payments. I listened to stories of success, stories of failure, stories of tragedies and stories of great achievements. Each person, regardless of stature, has a story to tell, and a great purpose in the world.

One of my favourite quotes came from Pope John Paul, as part of a speech he made when he visited Ireland in 1975. He said, 'You each have an important job'. 'You cannot do what I do, and I cannot do what you do', but this does not mean that my job is more important than yours, or yours than mine'. You see, so many of us admire somebody else's position, and think it is greater than ours. Some get side tracked and try to play the role of another. The truth is that each one of us have a different role to play in life. Whatever our role, the most important thing is that we do our absolute best to excel within our own role, whatever that may be. The greatest way to excel at any role is to approach it with love as the main ingredient. I remember a dinner lady in the canteen of one of our building sites in Birmingham. She would plop the food onto the plate with aggression, and shout 'next'. It was obviously a job that she didn't enjoy. Every plate to her was just a number in a line of workers waiting to be served. She dug the large spoon into the bain-marie and at whatever angle we held our plate, that's where the mash was slopped on, whether that was on top of the other food, or hanging off the side of the plate, and of course that was our fault, never hers. And we dare not ask for more. On her days off, another lady took her place, and even though it took a bit longer, she carefully made a quenelle with the spoon of mashed potatoes and placed it neatly on one side of the plate. She would have chopped parsley scattered on the top and asked us if we would like some more. Even though it was the same mashed potatoes, made by the same cook every day, the way this lady served the mash made it taste so much better. The plate looked better and even the atmosphere in the canteen was better. Our meal was more enjoyable, and every plate was empty before we left the canteen. Making the world a better place can be as simple as mash potatoes.

Did you know that the 2018 Global Wealth report from Credit Suisse Institute revealed that people with $4210 to their name are richer than 50% of the world's population? If you are one of these, you are blessed. You also have more opportunities than 50% of the world. You have the opportunity to invest it and increase it. The difference in the wealthier is that they use their money to make more money, whereas those who continue to spend what they have, continue to live paycheck to paycheck, week by week. Financial growth is only achieved by investing. I am not just talking about the stock markets or taking chances with the unknown. There are opportunities of all sizes for all budgets. It can be as simple as buying an old house and renovate it by doing most of the work yourself. It could take a few months, or even a few years. Then sell it to make a decent profit and use the profit to invest again. I remember a young woman who left home at seventeen due to difficult family problems. Her home was broken, and she had suffered abuse and neglect. It took great courage for her to leave, when she eventually found a friend that offered her a place to stay. To show her appreciation, she would clean her friends house and cook dinner every evening. When a neighbour would visit, they remarked on how clean the house was, and the difference she had made to the living room by moving furniture around and placing ornaments and accessories in different places. She created a less cluttered, more organized space, and improved the appearance so much that it added value to the house. The neighbour wanted the young girl to improve her home too. She gladly accepted the challenge and got handsomely paid. She had discovered her talent and was on the way to becoming a successful interior decorator. Three years later, she bought her own home, and continued to develop her business into a multimillion empire of cleaning and decorating services for homes across the country. She built a reputation and became one of the most sought-after designers of her time. I have great admiration for those who begin with nothing and achieve success through determination and consistence, regardless of their background.

There is a lot of talk about equality, and many interpret it wrongly. You see, we are not all equal and we never will be. Some of us are rich, and some of us are not. Some of us can be broke today and not tomorrow. Your mindset will determine your outcome, so you have a choice. I don't think that the man who lies in bed until lunchtime should have the equivalent of the man who gets up with the birds. I don't think that the man who downs tools at 5 o'clock and heads home to spend the evening watching Netflix should be rewarded the same as the man who spends his evenings making a second income or developing his business further. Some people are great at maths and others are great at languages. Some of us are dependent on others while some of us are independent. We need a variety of people to make up the world. We need people of all levels and talents to complement each other. Our attitudes and mindset are certainly not equal, and this will determine how we view and treat the people around us. It will determine how we see the world and where our priorities lie. We are all unequal in every area. Equality is for respect, love, and appreciation. Equality is for treating others as we expect to be treated ourselves, regardless of race, gender, or status.

Thomas Jefferson once said, 'Nothing can stop the man with the right mental attitude from achieving his goal'. He also said, 'Nothing on earth can help the man with the wrong mental attitude'. So, if attitude is so important, how can you tell if yours is good or not? Firstly, you must understand that it is not the mask you wear to present yourself to the world. It is the little things you mutter under your breath, which nobody else can hear. Is your dialogue one of blaming others or feeling sorry for yourself? Is it one of defence, thinking that the world is against you? Or is your dialogue one which makes you smile and count your blessings in any situation? What do you say to yourself when things go wrong? If you find yourself jumping into negative thoughts, then you may have a few disbeliefs that need to be changed. Making small adjustments to your attitude, can profoundly affect your life. People with good attitudes believe that the best will happen, but people with bad attitudes believe that the worst will happen. Either way, people tend to get what they expect.

Chapter 4

The Fruits of Success

I was brought up as a Catholic boy, where religion was taught in school, and we attended Mass every Sunday morning. Our clothes were washed and pressed to perfection to make sure we all looked our best. It was my job on a Saturday night to polish everyone's shoes for the next morning. I looked forward to it because the entire community gathered around the Church gates after Mass, and chatted for a while, so we all knew each other well. We looked forward to meeting up with all our friends and neighbours. Dances were held on a Sunday night, rather than a Saturday night, because the priest worried that we wouldn't be able to get up in time for mass the next morning. The priest attended the dances too. During a slow dance, if anyone got too close to another, they would feel a tip on the back from the priest reminding them to stay back a bit. During Mass, I heard so much about Jerusalem and all that had happened there. As a boy, it seemed like these places were a whole other world away, and I wished that I could visit someday and see all the places where the many bible stories happened. When my business was going well, and I had built a stable financial position for myself, I decided that now would be the perfect time to fulfil this dream. First, I took a flight to London, where I wanted to buy a video camera to record every moment of this once in a lifetime trip. I bought the latest most modern camera available at that time, which cost a lot. It worked with reels of film, which could be played back on a projectorscreen. This was my new toy, and I couldn't wait to use it. I admire technology and gadgets and always like to have the newest and best of them.

In 1977, my wife and I met with the group and tour guide in Birmingham with whom we had arranged to travel to the Holy Land. We travelled throughout the land, visiting the Sea of Galilee, in which I dipped my feet, walked around the Garden of Gethsemane, visited the stable in Bethlehem, and walked to the top of Mount of Calvary. I swam in the Dead Sea, the lowest land point on earth, which is 420m below sea level. I stood in the river Jordan, where John the Baptist baptised Jesus and many more. I visited the upper room where the Last Supper was held. I rode on a camel and walked across the border into Gaza. There were soldiers there, but it was easy to cross, as there was not much trouble at that time. In Gaza, there were little houses made of stone with open doors. The weather was hot, and the breeze blew the sandy dust around the streets. One local resident allowed me to come inside and see her home. She told me some stories about the war and all their troubles. My favourite stop was the City of David, the old city of Jerusalem. The old city walls stood withstanding the test of time. There were mounds of stones and boulders and so much evidence of historical events, all to support the old stories I had learned as a child. It was a magnificent place, steeped in history and culture. Many of the places remained untouched and stood the same as they were thousands of years ago. The narrow streets of cobble stones built by the Romans, were lined with the same old buildings, although some renovated to keep structurally sound. I had the pleasure of meeting a local gentleman called Ishmir. I was eager to learn more about the lifestyle here, so he brought me to a local bar in the old part of the city. It was a room dug into the rocks of limestone like a cave. The seats were bales of hay, scattered around the floor. The bar had its own homemade alcohol, undiluted and strong, which reminded me of the potin we used to make at home. We walked around the old streets and sat in an old café where the walls were rugged, and the ceiling was arched just enough to be able to walk through. The bartender boiled goats' milk to use for the coffee and served bread from the huge open fired oven. I felt like I was walking through those old times, taking the same steps of all those who had walked here before me, and even though in very different times, it was nostalgic and unforgettable.

‘Stop and take time to enjoy the fruits of your success’

Over time, I developed the factory, invested in new machinery, bought new vans, and trained new employees. I employed new salespersons and continued to grow at a steady pace. I built a second workshop, bigger and more modern than the first, with a huge storage loft and a new canteen. The local secondary school asked us to provide work experience for students. In fact, some of the students who came to us for the experience stayed with us and became great craftsmen. One evening when my digger driver was digging the site for my second workshop, he told me that he had just inherited a townhouse in Monaghan and didn’t want it for any purpose. Being the risk-taking character that I am, I took the spur of the moment decision and offered to buy it. We shook hands and I had just bagged myself another property. I didn't see it as a risk. It wasn't a huge amount of money, although a lot had to be spent to bring it to a modern liveable standard. The project became my hobby, and I relished the opportunity to get stuck into it. I transformed the old house into a beautiful three-story home ready for renting.

'Always take an opportunity during the lifetime of the opportunity' Eric Thomas.

I continued to grow my fireplace factory and gained a huge interest in the raw materials, their sources, varieties, and endless diversity. There was so much more I could do with these amazing slabs of marble and granite. With all the equipment and assets that I had, I further expanded my range and started the production of granite worktops for kitchens. I built good relationships with suppliers but noticed that my suppliers were becoming rich from my large orders, and because I was limited to colours and size depending on what my supplier would source, I was limited to what I could offer my customers. This is when I decided to source my own. My customers favourite choice at that time was a Portuguese marble, light cream in colour with a few flecks here and there, enhancing the natural beauty of the stone.

I took a leap of faith, jumped on a plane, and flew to Lisbon. I landed in Lisbon one Friday afternoon. With no idea where to go from there, I went straight to the information desk and asked the receptionist to point me in the direction of marble quarries. She told me about a village in the south of Portugal where marble blocks are quarried and cultivated. It was four hours away, so I hired a car and followed a map to the place she suggested. When the receptionist told me it was just a little village, she was very accurate. I arrived at a country village where there was only a tiny shop and a handful of houses, along a dusty road overlooked by mountains and burnt grass hedging. At the top of a hill ahead, I saw a castle with some activity. I drove up to the castle, which was a hotel, and secured a room for the night. All night I could hear clattering and banging but tried to ignore it and get some sleep. The following morning when I came down to the breakfast room, I heard two German tourists chatting about the noises of a ghost they had heard during the night. So, I ate my breakfast and left. I decided not to spend another night there after hearing their conversation. I approached the small village shop, where the attendant didn't have a single word of English. Neither of us could communicate a single word between us. I smiled and waved goodbye, and I knew I had arrived in the heart of rural Portugal, so I walked around for a while but couldn't find anyone who could help me. I drove around and a little further on near the coast I came to a tourist office, where eventually I found an English-speaking native. She was very helpful and came with me as an interpreter to an office just outside the village, where a group of companies had their base offices for their marble quarries. When I say offices, they were small stone buildings which cosmetically could be mistaken as old outhouses. I was met with dark skinned Portuguese men, with white dust scattered on their hair. They were friendly and welcoming and continued to speak in their native language, showing me samples of their produce. My interpreter did her best to keep up with their fast pace, as they offered us coffee and snacks. The owner of the quarry took us in his jeep up the steep hill of the mountain side. It was a dirt track with twisting bends getting steeper and moredangerous as we climbed. At one point, I looked out of the window to the wheels of the jeep flicking stones about 100ft down the mountain side every time he turned the wheel. I kept my eyes focussed ahead and comforted myself by the fact that this was a trip he made numerous times a day, and he hadn't fallen off the edge yet. The quarry was a magnificent sight. The machinery was bigger than I had ever seen, with huge 5m circular blades, all diamond tipped, spinning with water on the end of a what looked like a dozer. The driver drove the apparatus into the mountain to cut the marble blocks out of the mountain.

From there, the blocks were transported in lorries down the mountain to the factory, where they were sliced and polished to be prepared for export. I had certainly arrived at the right place. My interpreter left after I met one of the office guys who could speak my language. I got the full experience of marble and granite production. I could see for the first time how frustrating it was when customers asked these men to send them plain marble slabs without streaks. It just wasn't possible. This was a natural stone cut out of the mountain, and nobody could tell what colour or how many streaks and flecks it would have until it was taken and polished. This was one of the biggest challenges I faced with my customers. I took lots of photos and planned to get them developed into poster sized prints, frame them and decorated my showroom walls with them. So, every time a customer complained about a streak here and a fleck there, I could point to the wall and tell them they should have a word with God himself. I spent just over a week with these guys and began a new business relationship, which is still secure to this day.

When I returned home, I began preparations for the importation of my first container. I will never forget that day when the lorry arrived with the 20ft long container on the back, carrying 22 tons of marble slabs. I had hired a crane to offload them from the top and set them into place. It was a tight squeeze with the lack of yard space, and when the lorry was ready to depart, it couldn't get turned around. Of course, the other guys there stood scratching their head, saying 'We have a huge problem here', looking at me. They didn't realize that I had foreseen the problem from the moment the lorry had arrived and had already figured out a way around it. Using the crane, I lifted the trailer of the lorry about 50ft high into the air and turned it around ready to be hitched onto the cab, so it was facing the direction of the entrance. Whenever an obstacle or difficultly arose, my guys always stood there, stated the problem to me and waited to hear a solution. As their leader, it was expected of me to always have a solution. I called myself a leader, never a boss. I always thought that being called a boss, or calling myself a boss, gave me an upper hand and an authority, and I didn't like this status. I preferred to be called a leader, who led my team, rather than bossing them around. They

trusted my leadership and appreciated my respect for them. I
always gave them a responsibility according to their capabilities. I continually praised them, and they excelled in their work. I would walk around the factory and stand with each one of them for a few minutes, showing interest in their work, and in any personal stories they wanted to share with me. I would rub my hand down the piece of marble which they had just polished and tell them that nobody else could achieve this level of workmanship. They were proud of their work, so I was confident that each fireplace they produced would be done with pride and diligence. I am not saying that all my employees were perfect. I had many come, and many go just as quickly. I remember one in particular, who had a degree in engineering. To be honest I delighted at the idea of having an engineering graduate, and all the perks that would come with him, like the ability to repair a machine and I thought that his knowledge of tools and parts would be a great asset. The other upside would be that he wouldn't need much training which

was great at that time because the factory was so busy, and we needed someone who would be somewhat knowledgeable in advance. On his first day, I brought the graduate to the factory and showed him his first task, which was simply to cut a slab of marble to a particular size. Much to my horror, I discovered that the man could not read a measuring tape. He had never even held a measuring tape and couldn't tell the difference in centimetres and inches. He couldn't tell one end of a machine from the other. I couldn't believe it when the man became overwhelmed and said, 'Thank you for the opportunity, sir, but I can't do this work'. My belief in the education system decreased further. The man was a genius on paper but had absolutely no practical experience of any kind. A few weeks later I met him in our local deli wearing an apron and washing the dishes.

You should never rate people by a piece of paper.

The man should prove himself, rather than the paper approving the man.

In 2001, a monument was erected in Prince Edward Island, Canada, in honour of the Irish settlers who had emigrated there. Over ten thousand Irish citizens arrived there between 1767 and 1810, eventually making up over one quarter of the population on the island by 1850. I took an interest in the project, especially because of the huge number of emigrants that came from Co. Monaghan. Many of them came from Emyvale, Truagh, and parishes close to my homeland. They abandoned their cottages and lands in search of a better lifestyle. When I drive around these areas, close to my homeland, I see little stone cottages covered over with grass and bushes, and tress growing from the old stone chimneys. The land is fertile where it was once a family farm, full of fresh vegetables and happy families. I see the daffodils popping up in the Spring and think that somebody planted those bulbs many years ago, and they are still blooming and multiplying today. I proceeded to collect one piece of natural stone from the ground of each of the 32 counties in Ireland. We cut and polished each stone to size and placed them in a circular shape for installation on the memorial site on the island. Hundreds of tourists visit the monument every year and it serves as a reminder for all those who can trace back their ancestors to Ireland.

Everyone takes a holiday, and I was no different. When my family were young, I bought a caravan in early Spring, and we toured around the country visiting coastal towns and the scenic mountainous regions of Ireland. Each year we would choose a different region and spend a week relaxing and spending time with the children. We would park up at a site, set up the barbeque, and switch off from the rest of the world for a short time. There were no mobile phones then, so there were no disturbances. If there was an issue with my business back home, I wasn't contactable, so whatever happened, happened. I had no control over it, so I didn't think about it. Sometimes it's great to leave the world behind and spend a short while in simplicity and peace. We had good times and created lots of great memories. With the kids there was never a dull moment. When we returned from our break, I would sell my caravan to another family, and profit enough to cover the cost of our holiday.

Sometimes I took my family to Birmingham, and we would stay with my brother Michael and his family. Louis lived close by, and I loved spending time with them both. It was great being back and touring around the areas in which I had spent so much time during my younger years. I was amazed at how the areas where I once worked, had been so highly developed in such a short time. I enjoyed our visit to the Austin car factory in Longbridge. When I came home, I bought a 1934 Austin 7 car. I joined the vintage car club and drove through the parades in town on St. Patrick's Day. I still have the car and enjoy taking it for spins every now and again.

Take some time for yourself to look around and see the endless beauty which surrounds us. It doesn't have to be a lavish holiday abroad. I have watched families struggle and save for a holiday abroad every year, and they end up spending their years savings during their time away. They come home broke, and sometimes in debt. This is not a holiday; this is adding an unnecessary burden on yourself. The word holiday means an extended time of leisure. It doesn't require much money to give yourself some leisure time to spend with loved ones. The places you go should never outweigh the people you spend the time with, as this is all that matters. The greatest gift you can give to another is your time. I think that is one of the mistakes we all make in life, that we think we have plenty of time.

Always live within your means and don't spend money that you don't have. There are two types of debt. One is consumer debt, and the other is profitable debt. When you buy a car, expensive clothes, or anything for personal gain, it is considered consumer debt. This is money spent on items that only diminish or decrease in value. They are truly of no benefit. Profitable debt is when you use the money to invest into something that will create more wealth. Always keep your consumer debt to a minimum and reinvest your earnings into valuable assets that continue to grow and build wealth.

Chapter 5

A New Experience

In the early 1980's I was approached by an old friend, who told me about a new opportunity which had proven success and would yield financial freedom in every respect. It was a multi-level marketing business, based in the US, and because I was told that it only took a few hours a week to run, I decided to give it a go. Each member would have to sell products of all kinds, from household cleaners to jewellery and make-up, and there was something for everyone. To get another involved, there was a plan, which I had to explain to a prospective client by means of a whiteboard. I called to homes, preorganized, where groups of people gathered to watch me set up my whiteboard and begin showing the plan which was said to yield great profits. I excelled in sales, but I was also subjected to many negative comments and rejections, of which there were many. However, I carried on. The guys at the top of the ladder produced a range of positive thinking books and cassette tapes and encouraged all members to read and listen to them.   They hosted seminars, where they taught positive behaviours and told success stories. They reiterated that the rejections and negativity were inevitable and were necessary to filter suitable client prospects from the not so suitable ones. I bought and read many books, my favourite one being How to win friends and influence people. I have to say that the books really did increase my positive mindset and offered highly educational life stories and I learned a lot from them. When going on a car journey I would listen to the cassette tapes, covering goal setting, facing challenges and the explanations of mindset and how positive thinking overpowered negative thoughts, which hugely impacted one's success in all areas of life. This education was one of the best I had received, beyond that of any school or college. I thought that Attitude should be a subject placed as compulsory in all schools and colleges. I thought of nurses, doctors, and teachers, and how their attitudes and behaviours impacted our lives, especially those of children.

Milestones were set, and I had great admiration for the people at the higher levels. I travelled all over the country to hear them speak and to meet with them. They were inspirational, and very successful and I enjoyed being part of this organization. With determination and eagerness, I steadily rose to higher levels and eventually achieved good success, and with that, there came many perks. I was asked to run seminars and events. I remember standing on the stage in The Kings Hall in Belfast city, where I proceeded to give a lecture on how to be successful in sales to over 500 people. I kept it humorous, relatable, and educational. I was received with immense applause and appreciation. I was highly respected, and I had become one of the guys at the top. My reward for my achievements was an exclusive trip to the USA. I joined a group of likeminded people and headed off to tour the USA. We visited Miami, Florida, Seattle, and New York. We visited the Pocono Mountains in Pennsylvania where they were covered with snow. A tractor and trailer brought us up to the top and we took a slide to the bottom. My brother Patrick, (we called him Packie) had emigrated to Canada, so I took this opportunity to visit him and his family. We drove from Seattle to Vancouver and travelled on to his village, Mission. Packie was a nurse, and excelled in his field, eventually becoming a psychiatrist. He was an amazing guy, full of kindness and very much a family man. He was the only one in our family who had gone to secondary school, and he rode his bicycle every morning fourteen miles to get there. It was a fantastic trip and another amazing experience of a lifetime, of which I enjoyed every moment.

The business itself, although prosperous, was very challenging. I would have to down tools in my fireplace business at six o'clock in the evening, and quickly change before leaving home to make the three-hour car journey to Galway to host plans and give speeches to groups of clients. I wouldn't arrive home until the early hours of the following morning. The financial gain, although good, wasn't brilliant. I had greater expectations than that of which it yielded. Time was a huge factor, and I began to see the negative affect it was having on my fireplace business. The impact on the business I had spent so many years building, lead to my decision to leave the marketing behind and get my own business back on track. I could see that my absence caused a decline in progression, and things weren't running as smoothly as they should. However, I didn't see the marketing as a negative deterrent to blame. I saw it as a life experience from which I personally progressed and grew more confidence. I had met hundreds of great people, gave speeches to thousands, travelled some more of the world, and received a great education that would always stay with me.

I got my stone business back on track and continued to source raw materials from all over the world. On one of my trips to Italy, I stumbled across a stand at a trade fair, who were making granite tombstones, using almost all the same machinery and tools that I already had in my factory. Sure enough I needed to add some additional assets, but I saw this as another interesting venture which would perfectly fit into my existing production. So, I added another product to our portfolio. With little or no advertising, the tombstone business was thriving. With my building experience, the lining out and building of the foundation for the tombstone surrounds, was second nature to me. My granite kitchen worktop business was also thriving, and I purchased my very first CNC computerized machine which increased our production and quality immensely. With all that I had going on in the factory, we got busier and worked longer hours, most nights until midnight, and every weekend. Customers came from all over the country, and I built a large customer base of trade customers, who came to buy our products for resale in their own shops and outlets. We continued to add to our portfolio of products to include wood burning stoves, electric and gas fires, and all kinds of products associated with our niche.

When you start a new business or open a new shop, it starts with one item. I see many new shops opening and the owner wants to have the biggest and best property, with masses of stock. They want expensive décor and display areas of mirrored furniture and the most elaborate quality fittings. There is truly no need for this. Yes, you want your new shop to look great, but at what expense? Is it to keep up with the gift shop or the green café across the street who has been in business for twenty years or more? Start with little, and you can build on it over time. Only when your new business is up and running, you will find out which products yield the most profits and which ones are just not worth having. Keep it simple and decorate your new shop by painting it yourself and use DIY shelving. Buy used equipment where possible. I once walked into a small bakery shop, which a young lady had just opened. The floor area was big enough to hold only six customers at a time. The unplastered block walls were painted in olive green, and the unlevelled floor had been painted black. Tall wooden shelves, made of imperfect wood, held three different breads, which smelled divine. She had a tray of chocolate brownies on one side of the counter and a tray of apple sponge squares on the other. That was it! That was her offering. She had a selection of five baked products in total. However, her breads were exceptional. By 11am, her entire stock was sold. She continued baking throughout the day, in the one large oven at the back of her shop. The aroma was felt the whole way down the street, all day, which enticed passers-by to call in and make a purchase. She had developed an irresistible product, and built a customer base, which only increased over time. Shoppers would buy their groceries in the large supermarkets in the area and come into this tiny bakery to get their bread. The ambience and simplicity of the shop created an organic atmosphere, superior to that of the supermarket chains, which took millions of dollars to open, with an endless selection of breads. The bakery lady would make one tray of new products once a week. Her devout customers would give her honest feedback, as she would consider adding to her range. In most cases, less is best, and simplicity is the best way to start.

According to the US Bureau of labour Statistics, 20% of new businesses fail in the first two years, and 45% fail within the first five years. Only 25% make it beyond fifteen years. The most common cause is lack of cash flow. They thought they would become successful overnight, but it takes time. They put all their money into lavishness and don't get a return on their investment fast enough to keep the business running. They have too many offerings which can be confusing and overwhelming for customer choice. When I started, I was making fireplaces in a garage. It took two years to gain the financial stability to build a new workshop. It took a further two years to build a showroom, and so on. I took each step one at a time, knowing for sure that I had a market, and knowing what my customers wanted most. I kept my designs to a minimum, and the structures within the capabilities of the staff and machinery that I had. I never complicated the sale by saying to the customer, I can put a rounded edge on this side or different shapes on that side. This would only cause difficulties for my staff, and delays for my customers. What they see is what they will buy. Quality is what matters most. Supply and Demand are the key words here. I once bought in slabs of marble, which to me were beautiful, but they didn't sell. You see it's not what I think is nice that matters, it's what sells. There must be a demand, and this will be evident in the first two years. I have seen new products of all kinds, and some very innovative ideas, but the demand wasn't there, and they never took off.

All this goes for an online business too. Marketing gurus and website builders will entice you to go for the biggest and most elaborate website pages, beyond what is necessary. If your product is in demand, the expensive software tools will serve the same purpose as the simple ones. It is always quality over quantity. A two-page website can yield as much as a ten page one. In fact, too many pages and too many options will confuse the customer. I hear younger start-ups saying, I can't put up a website without top notch links, new logos, and a perfect colour scheme. This attitude results in the lengthy, time consuming and expensive building and developing of sites, while you take your focus off what really matters. You can become engrossed in the details that force your mind to wander away from the purpose of the task. Then some will attend courses and workshops, thinking it is necessary to have all this knowledge. Never take your eye off the ball. Let the website builders build the websites, while you work on your business. You would never see a fireman trying to design and stitch his own armour. He is too busy fighting fires, so he lets the tailor stitch the suit.

Another important point is to always do right by your brand. I remember speaking with a Jewish gentleman who had went to a printing shop to get some work done. When he walked into the shop the walls were decorated with Christian images and there were religious booklets sitting alongside the printing materials. The gentleman became uncomfortable and decided to take his business elsewhere. The printing shop had portrayed the wrong image for their brand. They discouraged anyone outside of their own personal faith to do business with them. This immediately limited their customer base. I believe in separating your business from your personal matters. I believe that each customer should be respected for who and what they are, and your own beliefs and choices should be kept personal. It is important to make every customer feel welcome and not categorized or judged. This way we show respect and acceptance and our willingness to do business with all people from all walks of life and this is how we promote our brand.

I remember a man who started a new health food shop and he promoted weight loss products. He had a little weight on himself, and he would be seen sitting on a chair behind the counter devouring chocolate cakes and sweets. When a customer would come in for weight loss advice, he would hide them under the counter and proceed to talk about healthy eating habits and exercise. Customers are smart and not easily fooled. You must practice what you preach and be living proof that your product is worth it. You are your brand, and you must live it. Can you imagine the outcome if this man had taken his own advice? And how much more would he have excelled in business if he had become fit and healthy and stand in his shop with a 'before and after photo' of his personal progress through the plans and products he was promoting? However, his business closed within twelve months.

One morning, I had to make a call in Cavan town, about 30 miles away, where I had to measure a shop front for granite facing. The rain poured down profusely that morning in bouts of showers. As I held my measuring tape along the plinth of the shop, the showers began again. This time it was heavier. I ran across the street and stood in a doorway, huddled with a few others. I stood beside an older man who started complaining about the rain. He said he was the owner of this shop, which he had owned and worked in, for the last 30 years. He said, 'I am getting older, and fed up with running this shop for so long and would love a change'. I took a quick glance around and sympathized with the man. We continued to talk, mostly about doing the things that make us happy in life. To make a long story short, the man and I shook hands, as I agreed to buy his shop. I gave him a lifeline, to sell up and live the life he wanted, while I seized an opportunity to open a new fireplace outlet in Cavan town. It was a big town, equal to that of Monaghan, and with no fireplace shop within a 30-mile radius, mine was the first of its kind. Isn't it amazing what opportunities come our way in the midst of an unwelcome heavy shower of rain!

'Always remember that every day is a great day, whatever the weather, and opportunities are waiting on every street corner, even in the pouring rain'

After decorating the shop, and filling it with fireplaces and stoves, I approached my youngest brother, Francie. Francie had previously been in the building trade and was highly experienced in his field. He had many contacts in the construction sector, so I asked him if we would run the business in Cavan.

He agreed. Francie excelled in his management of the Cavan outlet. With the assistance of his wife, he sourced and purchased giftware, and continue to add new lines to enhance the business. He was competent, capable, and very thorough. He was a great salesman and gained much business for the company. His reputation and upstanding character secured good business relations with builders and customers alike. After Francie's retirement, the shop declined somewhat in sales, and many years later, there are still customers who ask about him.

Personal relationships are the life and breath to every success and achievement.

I went on to open many other outlets and smaller production units including Ardee, Galway, Wexford, Northern Ireland and more. These outlets were taken over by the property owners, and run privately which worked well, because I could continue putting my efforts into my factory, while they continued to sell produce, all sourced from me.

By helping others, you also help yourself

I was driving through the village of Glaslough, a small village in Monaghan, famous for its Castle, with magnificent grounds of gardens and lakes. The old castle, now a hotel, dates back to 1665, and has been well maintained with displays of valuable artifacts and antiques. Many celebrities, including Paul Mc Cartney held their wedding here. The village itself has gained many awards in the tourism sector and the best of the tidy towns events. I stopped at the only shop in the village to grab a bottle of water. I knew the lady behind the counter, as I had installed a fireplace in her home a short time prior. Herself and her husband had been running this small shop for many years. We started talking and after a few minutes I could see that she wanted to leave her current way of life to spend more time with her husband and family. When I showed an interest, she gave me a tour of the shop and the small outhouses that came with it. Once again, I saw an opportunity. When I offered to buy the shop, the lady was delighted and arranged for a second meeting where I secured a lucrative deal with herself and her husband to purchase the shop. This business was a little different from my usual interests. Due to the age and the depth of history with the village, all the buildings were protected. This factor alone made the investment more attractive. The building was old, and the shop turnover was small. However, this was not surprising as the shop had very little to offer in the way of fresh produce. I spent a lot of time and effort redecorating and transforming the shop into a great community asset. Over the years, I added a café upstairs, and more recently developed the outhouses into magnificent storerooms. I added a gelato making unit, and a fabulous gelato bar. The shop is now much more than a shop. It is a welcome asset to the Glaslough community as well as for tourists and visitors. When a townhouse next door to my shop went up for sale, I bought that too. I figured it would be an additional asset, and because it was located next to the shop, it would make perfect accommodation for the staff.

The shop brought many challenges too. With the strict planning laws of the village, I was tied in many ways, and had a lot of red tape to get through. The food business was a whole new sector, which I knew little to nothing about. When they health inspectors arrived, some of the work I had done had to be redone. Now I could understand why the previous owners had done little to modernize the shop and sell fresh food. All the rules and regulations seemed overwhelming, but for me, they were possible to achieve. Whenever my plans were rejected, I looked for another way. I never try to jump over the hurdles that were made of brick walls. Instead, I looked for gaps and weakness in the wall, which I could easily break through to get to the other side.

'Never give up' – Where there is a will, there is always a way'

One morning when busy in the factory moving pallets with the forklift, I was approached by a well-dressed man in a suit, carrying a briefcase. I climbed down off the forklift in my dusty jacket and work boots to greet him. His professional look and official tone of speech suited his purpose well. This was my first encounter with a health and safety officer who had come to cause trouble. He pulled out a little handheld computerized gadget and said he was here to take noise level readings. 'Noise level readings', I thought. What nonsense is this? Every machine made a noise, and the more noises they made, the more production was happening, the more fruit I was yielding, and the more employment I was providing. This man certainly didn't have the best interest at heart for our business. He was one of those authority figures who worked on a set of rules and regulations made up by a group of college graduates who had absolutely no experience in how to a run a business and they certainly didn't care. Regardless of the consequences, and without a single thought for the families that depended on a week's wages, most of these Inspectors had more authority than I appreciated, and they continued to abuse it. The well-dressed official proceeded to show his authority and held his little gadget over every machine and area of my factory. 'This is too loud', he would say. 'This one is also too loud', he said. 'Put a guard on this machine' he said. 'Pick up that piece of marble and put it in its place'. I watched and listened as the man proceeded to check that the toilets were flushing correctly and that that the workers quarters were in line with that of a five-star luxury hotel. My workers became agitated as their happy space became invaded by this overbearing stranger. When he was finished his report, we went to the office to talk about his findings. He listed several changes we needed to make to bring the factory up to the required levels of the health and Safety standards. He proceeded to reveal that the local authorities had received a complaint from some of the neighbours, that we were creating noise pollution in a residential area. He produced paperwork, made demands, and gave us some time to have them implemented. For the protection of the business, I worked with my team, and we implemented all the necessary changes needed to be compliant and be ready for his next inspection. To keep my neighbours at bay, I planted some trees, fitted new reinforced doors, and kept the noise to a minimum as best I could. However, the complaints continued. The neighbours became a problem. They complained about how we stored our stone, where we stored our gas cylinders, and too many cars coming and going. It was never-ending. It was obvious that it wasn't going to stop. As frustrating as it was, I chose not to get angry. I would meet my neighbours and speak well to them. I never mentioned the complaints and continued to greet them respectfully. Yes, I am human, so yes, it was hard to smile, but I chose not to lower my standards or allow anyone to decide my mood or to upset my day. There is a time to be quiet and a time to speak. The spoken word can create wars. A war needs an opposition to begin. When the first shot is fired, they are waiting on a reaction. The smartest person in the room stays quiet and waits until everyone else say their piece. This gives him time to think, and time to reflect on what the rest are saying. You see thinking on the spur of the moment is a spontaneous reaction, but a patient mind is responsive. A patient mind will weigh up the situation and is more likely to come up with a positive solution. Always be in charge of your own mind and choose never to react. A wise man keeps his thoughts to himself and will reveal them in the form of a solution when the time is right.

The higher you raise your head above the crowd, the more eggs will get fired at your face.

Through it all, I still never gave up my hobby of buying and selling property. One sale in particular still makes me smile to this day. I remember sitting in the solicitor's office with the buyer, ready to sign the last piece of paperwork, when he said, 'Hang on a second, I have a small problem'. I turned to him and waited to hear what it was. 'I have no money' he said. The solicitor and I looked at each other with shock, and the room was silent for a few moments. 'I have 20 acres of farmland in nearby Glaslough, and I will give you that instead', he said. I sat in silence for a few moments before I agreed. I really didn't want the land, but this man needed a family home. Things don't always go our way in life. The most important thing to remember is that no matter how difficult things are for us, there is always another person in greater need. I believe that when we get the opportunity to help another person to achieve their goals, or simply help them through a difficult time, we will be rewarded greatly later in life.

'Always treat others with patience and understanding. Each of us encounter good times and hard times, and when hard times arise, we hope there will be a kind-hearted hand to reach forward and help us out'

I enjoyed my new farm of land for a short while. I bought cattle to graze on the green grass and employed a local man to look after it. There was a little stream with lots of wildflowers growing on its banks. Every time I heard the bumble bee buzzing around, it reminded me of harvest time at home when my mother brought food up to the hayfield. Back then the bumble bees were plentiful, as were so many other forms of nature, which I rarely see or hear anymore. We used to catch the grasshoppers and watch the corncrake building its nest secretly in the hay and when I came home late at night after a party, I would know I was almost home when I could hear the corncrake in our hayfield. Their rasp was loud and distinctive At that time, we cut the hay with a scythe, and we would carefully avoid the nests. However, when the modern machinery and tractors were brought in, the nests were destroyed, so they slowly became extinct. When I was approached by a local farmer who wanted to buy the land, I agreed, and made twice the profit I would have made from getting paid for the house. My willingness to compromise had paid off, so it was a winning situation for us all. I bought another farm of land from an elderly lady who lived on her own. She had inherited land and was not physically able to look after it. She had no money and lived in the old cold farmhouse by herself. I was there to advise her on a new stove for heating, and after spending some time with her, I bought her land and helped her to make the necessary changes to achieve a happier and warmer home. I bought some deer to graze on the land and enjoyed them for a while. When I put a stag in with the dear, it was a danger zone during the mating season. Being brought up on a farm had taught me to never mess with the male animal during mating season. I would watch a bull from a distance and become apprehensive at his unpredictable aggression. He would kneel on his front legs and dig the ditches with his horns. His huge muscular body and powering strength would wage war on anyone invading his territory. I remember being sent to the well when I was a kid and had to walk through the field to get there. I would be weary and keep checking to make sure there was no sign of the bull. When I was coming back with the water, I could see him in the distance, scrapping at the ground and ripping at the hedge with his horns. I quickly headed back the other way, and took a two-mile detour to get home, where they all thought that I had fallen into the well. Maybe all my fond memories of farming at home was one of the reasons why I bought many other farms and properties of all different sizes, which I eventually sold and yielded good profits.

Chapter 6

Building an Empire

One evening when I was driving home from a job, the issues of my neighbours' complaints were on my mind, and I needed a way to get rid of these complaints once and for all. I drove past a large field with an old derelict house and some outhouses. With a stream running down along one side, I stopped to admire it. It was positioned on the outskirts of a village called Clontibret, about 3 miles from home. With no houses in the vicinity and being within a short distance to some furniture factories, I thought, what an ideal location to build a new factory. I had found a solution. The previous years I had spent working day and night, had allowed me to be in the perfect financial position to build a new factory, bigger and better than the one I already had. I had just created a new goal. Before I got excited, I approached my long-standing architect, and talked about the possibility of getting planning permission in that area. With a positive outcome, I didn't hesitate in seeking out the owner of the field and I purchased it. After sifting through lots of red tape, it took me twelve months to build the factory. It was an amazing achievement, perhaps one of my greatest. I incorporated 2 showrooms, several offices, and a huge workspace, second to none. I installed the latest high-tech machinery, and it became one of the biggest stone processing facilities in all of Ireland. Slowly production came to an end in the old yard, but I kept and maintained it for storage. I now had the space for containers of any size. Lorries could easily come and go. The health and Safety officer wouldn't have to write as many notes in his little black book. Production excelled to great levels. I watched van and lorry loads of goods leaving the factory. We were making fireplaces like hot cakes, and never seemed to have enough. Our employment levels grew, as well as my assets. In a way, I must thank my neighbours for all the complaints that came my way. If they had not persisted, I would not have taken the action so soon to acquire my new factory. I always believe in always taking the positive out of a negative situation. There is always a positive, you just need to be patient and focused to figure it out and the penny will drop.

'For every adversity in life there is always an equal or better opportunity.' Napoleon Hill.

I continued to travel throughout Europe and attended trade fairs to buy new raw materials and keep up to date with the latest technology and machinery. I met with quarry owners in Belgium, France, Germany, Italy, Portugal, and Spain. I made lifelong friendships and took advantage of my trips to explore all the different cultures and lifestyles. In Italy, I admired the spectacular architecture evident across the country. I was amazed at the huge mounds of stone standing tall at the Arena in Verona. With the lack of machinery back then, it is a mystery to me how they got those huge stones mounded so high and perfectly positioned. The structure was built in 30 AD to host events for up to 30,000 spectators. It is steeped in history and was the place where wild animals were placed to fight against people for entertainment. It has been restored after an earthquake caused extensive damage in 1117 and is now used to host more humane events today like operas and concerts. I admired the buildings in Rome, where some of the world's greatest artists achieved magnificent works of architecture, paintings, and sculptures, my favourite being those of Michael Angelo. I visited the Colosseum, The Sistine Chapel, and many more famous sites, as well as the endless Mediterranean beaches. I enjoyed the pizzas and the fresh olives and the Italians love for food and wine. I remember the beautiful outdoor cafes and restaurants which lined the streets and wondered how they all thrived so well in business with so much competition on their doorstep. I approached a restaurant to read the menu on display and the waiter asked me what my preference was for lunch. He said, 'If you would like to eat fish, my good friend Marco next door makes the best fish in Italy'. If you prefer red meat, then go two doors down to Alberto. He has the most tender beef you could imagine. If you prefer chicken, then come right in because our chicken is the best'. I immediately understood how the Italians didn't see competition as an issue. They embraced it and used it to their advantage. Each of the restaurants complimented each other and promoted each other. In the evenings they would take turns to dine in each other's restaurants and come up with new ideas. What a genius way to turn competition into an asset and make it your friend. I often heard the saying that the Italians love to eat, while the rest of the world eats to live. This was so evident, as the workers took two hours for lunch during the summer, so they wouldn't have to work at the hottest hours of the day. They met with family and friends and their lunch was a feast of food. Unlike us Irish, who usually swallow our lunch as fast as possible to get back to work, the

Italians took the two hours to eat and drink at their leisure.

In Portugal, I sat at a café with my marble supplier, at the foot of the Estrela Basilica, where the tram stopped before making its way back up the steep cobblestone slopes of the city. It was beautifully warm, and diners all ate and drank outside at marble mosaic tables, sipping coffee and Portuguese cream tarts. It was here that I tasted Kind prawns for the first time. They were served cold, on ice, with a serving of sea salt. The head and body were still intact. My marble supplier kindly demonstrated how to firstly pull the head off, then using his two thumbs, peeled back the shell and use the silver scraper to remove the digestive tract. He dipped the prawn into the sea salt, squeezed over some lemon and place it into his mouth. He closed his eyes and his expression really proved how much he enjoyed that prawn. He guided me on my first try. Much to my surprise they were undoubtedly delicious. To this day I have never tasted prawns as delicious as those I had on that beautiful summers evening in Lisbon.

Business was good in Ireland at that time, not just for me but for the whole country. These times were labelled as the Celtic Tiger years and the banks gave loans and mortgages to almost anyone. The building trade was booming, and thousands of houses were being built across the country. Inflation rose, and house prices rose to their highest of all time. Building sites and commercial land were being sold for sky high unjustified prices. When the banks offered me loans at low interest rates, I remembered my father's lesson about not confusing price with value, so I decided to use any accumulated funds to invest in new machinery and add to my assets instead. Almost everyone I knew, whether a plumber or a carpenter, bought a second house during these booming times. Builders paid millions of Euros for pieces of land, which a few years previously would have cost less than a quarter of this. It didn't make sense to me. The banks threw out huge loans to businesses and individuals alike, with very little collateral behind them. In 2008, the recession hit, and it hit hard. The property prices dropped dramatically, almost overnight.

Those who had bought a house at 300,000 were in serious trouble as their house was now only worth less than half that amount. Imagine the trouble hundreds of people encountered as the land they had purchased was worth so little now and they would never be able to recoup their investments. I heard many sad stories of severe losses, resulting in suicide. Empty properties, rows of unfinished houses, and empty pockets left them broke. Divorce rates doubled, as did our taxes to bail out the banks who had no funds behind their promises. A few months after the downturn, a local builder approached me to ask if I would buy two houses which he had left unsold in a development he had built. I was reluctant at first, but the man was on his knees, like many others, and needed to get out of the building business. He was emigrating the following week and said that if I didn't buy these two properties, they would be repossessed by the finance company. The man was in desperation, so I went with him to view the houses, and I bought them. For me it was a great investment, at a knockdown price. They were fine 3-bedroom houses with excellent rental potential. I was one of the few to be in a better financial position than most, to take advantage of the buyers' market. Today, the houses are worth five times what I paid for them.

Sales slowed down considerably, but my business survived and kept afloat at a steady pace. I had made the right decision not to invest in the ridiculously high-priced property ventures and because I had invested in my business instead, I was now reaping the rewards. Every machine and piece of stock I owned, were mine. I owed nobody anything. I wasn't in debt and therefore in a sustainable position to continue as usual.

'The business world is full of greed. Plenty who know the price of everything, and the value of nothing'

I read a synonym once about a train. When you place a penny on a train track in front of the wheel, the train won't move, but if you put a penny on a train track while the train is going at one hundred miles an hour down the track it will hit the penny and tear it apart into pieces. I felt this described my business well. Over the years I had built an empire. It became unstoppable. It was now running itself. It has many valuable assets, a long-standing customer base, trained and dedicated staff, and a reputation of high standing. All my years of dedication, the sleepless nights, the sacrifices and the many aches and bruises from climbing all the solid brick walls, had yielded their rewards. When I look back, I can honestly say that my years of struggle were the best years of my life. I am sure you have often heard that Rome wasn't built in a day. The Israelites were 400 years in slavery before they reached the edge of the promised land. It took Moses forty years to lead his group of people to the promised Land. On the journey, thousands of people died. They moaned and groaned and became frustrated. They lacked patience. The journey became too difficult and so many of them gave up. They lost faith in themselves and in their leader. There were days they had no food, but there were days they had plenty. It is still the same for us today. Some days will be good, and others will be challenging. This makes the good days great days. It makes our achievements more worthwhile. No matter what struggles we face in life, always be the one who climbed the tallest wall. Be the one who makes the world a better place for yourself and for others around you and never give up the fight.

It is never the size of the man; it is the size of the fight in the man that counts.

My physical work slowly decreased, and I could come and go as I pleased. I continued to lead the business, but in a less physical way. I could also spend more time enjoying my hobbies, and my grandchildren. I could go for walks in the evening, which I thoroughly enjoyed. I would take an hour or two alone, enjoy the fresh air away from the hustle and bustle of it all. It was invigorating and a quiet stress-free time. Even though I had made many friends over the years, I realized that I had not one genuine friend whom I could trust unconditionally. My friends over the years were great friends, and during our short friendships, we made many memories and had unforgettable great times.

I learned not to be too expectant of others and to always rely only on myself. Relying too much on a somebody else can lead to disappointment and fallouts. I also never needed someone else approval. I am proof enough of who I am and what I have achieved. Friendships need to be nurtured, not abused. There are two sure ways to fall out with a friend. One is to lend, and the other is to borrow. When sharing a success moment, one friend said to me, 'Its alright for you, you have the money to do what you like'. His statement revealed a lot about his attitude. He failed to see the sacrifices and commitment I had made to achieve it. He had decided that I was in a better position than him to make it, but the truth was that he had made his own choices, which lead to where he is today, like my old friend who wouldn't come and gather potatoes with me in Northern Ireland, so that we could buy a new bicycle. In a way, he begrudged me of my success. We all have a choice whether to decide on doing what it takes to succeed or to decide that what it takes to succeed is too much hassle and simply not worth the effort.

‘A pessimist will see difficulty in every opportunity, but an optimist will see opportunity in every difficulty’

Chapter 7

Be Your Own Hero

Have you ever heard of a self-starter? Its like a crank shaft. I remember having to turn the crank shaft on my first car to make it start. Some people remind me of a crank shaft. They need to get a kick, or a nudge to get going. They lack self-motivation and tend to thrive on the glory from others to gain admiration. It's like a question one from one of my favourite speakers which he asked during a seminar one evening. He asked the crowd, 'If I gave you the choice of being the president of the

United States for a day, or give you a million dollars, which would you choose?' With a show of hands, the overwhelming majority chose to be the president of the United States for a day. I was taken back by this. I couldn't understand why so many enjoyed admiration and honour from others. The opinions of others didn't bother me. I was always a self-motivator. I was my own hero and if others liked or disliked me, it was none of my concern. What others say about me is none of my business. In fact, if we all knew what others spoke about us, and took it to heart, I am not sure if anyone would be speaking to anybody. There will always be people against you. There will always be people to speak negatively about your actions and intentions. I believe it is jealousy, or a fear that if you succeed it will make them look bad. In most cases, the best way is to keep your intentions to yourself, and you can share your success when it is achieved. This way you will only have yourself to answer to.

'Wish all your enemies a long life, so they can see you succeed'

Remember, no one is coming to save you. No one is coming to do it for you. No one is really bothered whether you succeed or not. Sometimes not even your own family. Do it for yourself. Associate with those who have only your best interest at heart. Find likeminded people within the same field and watch and listen to how they did it. Feed yourself with positive and motivational materials, through books, videos, or any of the many other sources available. A positive mindset is vital and through it all, never take your mind off the end goal. Put your goal as the picture you see first thing when you wake up in the morning. Place a photo or caption of your goal on the screen saver of your phone, or on the dashboard of your car or any place that you will see often. It will continually remind you that you are working towards it. Whenever you feel elated, or tired, look at the picture and remind yourself that you are worth the effort.

Get a notepad and write down your goals. You need to list three types.

The first is The Short-Term Goal

This goal is one you set when you decide to take action on a particular project. Set a goal to reach your first achievement. It should be simple and easy to reach. It could be as simple as losing 5 pounds, or if setting up a new business, it could be to have all the paperwork and red tape investigated and overcome.

The second is The Long-Term Goal

This goal is the one you set to reach within 12 months. Don't be so lenient with this one. The first twelve months of anything new is the most important. This is when the foundations are built, which are the most important part of any business.

The third is The Ultimate Goal

This goal is the reason that you set the first two goals. This goal is the one that you most want to achieve in life. It could be three years away, five years away, or even ten.

In between the three main goals, you will set intermediate goals. These will be necessary so that you stay focussed and stay on track to achieve the others. Always focus on the Ultimate goal and remember that it is ok to change direction. Sometimes we take the wrong path in life and get a little lost. Sometimes we make a decision that didn't yield the results we expected. However, that is fine, and you shouldn't lose heart. Its not about how many times you fall, its about how many times you get back up after you fall and keep going. Remember, how did the man eat the elephant? One bite at a time. If you reach any of your goals sooner than expected, be proud, and reward yourself. Always do a little more than expected.

This reminds me of the story of a young boy who lived in the same estate as a professional golfer. The golfer was famous and had won many titles. The young boy wanted to become a professional golfer also. One evening after school, he approached the man and asked him if he would teach him all the tricks and moves to becoming great. The professional willingly agreed and said to the boy, If you want to become a successful golfer like me, you have to train hard. Meet me on the course at 7am every morning and I will train you for two hours before you go to school, and on Saturday mornings at 7am and we will train for four hours. The young boy said Hey, I'm not going to get up that early every morning and I am not going to give up my Saturdays playing with my friends. Well then, said the golfer, you will never become like me. The young boy walked away. He had given up on his dream because he wasn't prepared to pay the price for success.

I once heard Ronald Regan say that self-discipline is the most important skill that a parent can teach a child. From I was a boy, I was given chores and there was no such thing as saying, 'I'll do it later'. If a job needed doing, it was done there and then. There was no such thing as saying that the job was too hard, or I am too tired to do it. This resulted in self-discipline that came naturally. When 6am arrived, we would get out of bed automatically, without being called, because it was the done thing. We knew what we had to do, and we just did it. I believe that this is the reason that I was capable of leaving my parents at

16, to fend for myself in the huge cities of England. I was just a boy from rural Ireland, who had never been to a city before. I was independent. I didn't need someone to waken me in the morning and tell me it was time to go to work. I didn't need anyone to tell me to save my money to have enough to pay my rent every week. I fed myself, I cooked and cleaned for myself, and I managed my finance myself. I see college students coming home at the weekends with a basket of laundry for their parents to do. They will spend the weekend with their friends and put out their hand for their parents to feed them and pay the rent for the following week. This only creates dependence and expectations which limits their ability to learn the value of money, and how it is earned. On the other hand, a student who has to work in the evenings and at the weekends to provide for themselves are much less likely to fail their exams and miss classes. They gain an understanding of the value of money and are much more cautious of how they spend it. They become independent, responsible, and mature. They make better decisions and are much more likely to succeed.

I heard little or nothing of mental health issues, until my later years in life. In my younger years, only the disabled people were considered disadvantaged. I remember one man in our home community who walked through the fields talking to himself. He may have had some brain malfunction disorder, but he still worked like the rest of the farmers and was never treated differently. Today I hear much about mental illness and depression. But what is it really? It is a state of mind. It is your thoughts. It is your perspective on the world around you. Let's be honest here, you have pathed the way to where you are today. But the good news is that you can change your situation, no matter how big of a pickle you have gotten yourself into. If it is debt, there is an office in every city, like MABS here in Ireland. They are there for the purpose of helping you to pay off your debts according to your means. In some cases, they can even help you to write off some of them. There are numerous options, but never ignore a problem or a situation because it will fester and sometimes multiply. There is always a way forward. Never give up on yourself and continue to seek a solution. Worrying won't solve anything, it will make things worse and damage your health. Take hold of your life and demand it to become great. Just remember that an idle mind can be a dangerous one, so you must continue to set goals, you must continue to work to reach those goals, and make sure that you love what you are doing. When you are feeling deflated, think of a great place you want to visit and visualize it. If it is Miami beach, then picture yourself there, relaxing on a deck chair, sipping champagne. Then go ahead and book the flight, even if it is one or two years away, just book it. You now have something to work towards, and your mindset will change. To maintain our inner happiness, we must keep achieving. I guess that is why most winners of the lottery blow their money fast, and don't appear to be as happy as we would have expected. You see money doesn't buy happiness. Happiness is always within yourself, no matter what you have. Yes, money is of huge importance in our lives, and without it we would be very unhappy. You can buy a house, but not a home. You can buy a bed, but not quality sleep. But achieving, reaching goals, and creating something from nothing, are all forms of winning. When we win, we are on top of the world. Eighty seven percent of millionaires in the world started with nothing. This is proof that it is about mindset. Whoever gets money handed to them, doesn't appreciate it the same. I once heard a millionaire saying that he would leave his children nothing, because if they can't make money on their own, how are they going to know how to look after his.

The unhappiest person in the world, has nothing to look forward to

Now, I also understand that there are some genuinely sad cases, especially in young people, who are being severely bullied or severely suffering from a poor self-image. Social media plays a huge part in this. Social media, like alcohol or drugs, only becomes a problem when it is abused, and overused. All these things have their purpose and are important for progression. As the world changes, we must change with it, or we will be left behind. The advancements in technology have progressed significantly, and they are there to enhance our lives and our businesses. We should use them for the purpose of progression, and fit them into our lives as an asset, for the right reasons. Never do or say anything that has no positive benefit for yourself or for others around you. Delete offensive material or anything that doesn't offer benefit for your self-progression. Follow those who are likeminded, and the sites and pages that offer education and enjoyment within your own interests. Don't ever follow another just for the sake of it because their posts will become a distraction and you will veer off the path that you want to follow.

When I was a kid, we would catch flees and trap them into a jam jar and seal the lid. The flees would jump up and down and hit the lid and we kept them trapped for days. When we opened the lid, we expected them to fly out, but they didn't. They had become accustomed to jumping to the level of the lid, and even with the lid off, they continued to jump to that same level. It became their comfort zone. It became normal to them, and they never reached any higher. Choose your friends wisely. You will be influenced by them. If they are negative and have a negative outlook, this will rub off on you. The young are too open and willing to engage with wrongdoers, because of their nature to discover new things and new behaviours.

A twelve-year-old girl, who had been taking ballet classes from she was four years old, loved her ballet and her favourite day of the week were the days on which she had her classes. In the later years of primary school, when most children begin their social media profiles, her friends put up photos of themselves playing football and winning trophies. The talk was all about football and she felt left out. She would hear an odd remark, and an odd snigger here and there about her dancing and how it just wasn't cool. She didn't want to be singled out as being different and it saddened her not to be part of this group. The young girl left her dancing and joined the football team. She spent twelve months training and going to matches, and even though she enjoyed the crack and being part of the group, she became very unhappy within herself. She had sacrificed her own dreams, just to be a part of others. She learned a very valuable lesson. She eventually left the football, re-joined her ballet group, and decided to never lose sight of her own dreams again.

Don't let anyone steel your dream – Better to live like a lonely lion, than with a bunch of sheep

I knew a man from Monaghan who had a very successful business of cutting and supplying raw materials for the furniture industry in Monaghan. He was around the same age as myself and like me, he had always used the imperial system of feet and inches. When the metric system became more popular, he refused to change. He would only accept orders placed in the old method of using feet and inches. When orders would come in, he sent them back and demanded they be resent in feet and inches. Over time, the orders stopped coming. He made a huge loss and eventually had to close his business. Always embrace change, keep learning, and keep up with the times, or you will be left behind.

Change is inevitable, growth is optional

For some, the word investment sounds scary. For some it means the stock markets, or the unreachable big companies dealing in millions. The definition of investments in the dictionary is using money to gain profits. For me it means being fruitful. Time is also an investment. It starts by planting a small seed, which is the thought or idea in your mind. The seed you choose will determine the type of fruit it will produce. Think about the fruit, before you choose the seed, with your ultimate goal being your reason of choice. Don't choose a sunflower seed and expect it to yield strawberries. Focus on your goal here, and then choose the correct seed to produce it. In between the seed and the fruit is the journey. This is the time and effort you will invest through hard work, and perseverance. Just like a plant or a tree, you will nurture your seed through knowledge using the appropriate tools. For a plant, you would use the most fertile soil, buy the best plant food, and water it every day. When the first little shoot comes up from the ground, you will be in awe at its progression. You will watch it grow and delight in all its beauty, continually adjusting to its needs, like changing it into a bigger pot, or adding more fertilizer. You will grow and change with every step of its progress. Now if the little shoot doesn't appear when it should, this is not a failure. This is merely an indication that you have done something wrong. You would never give up on the idea, so you start again. The little setback was a learning experience. Make sure that you do learn though. I have seen people repeating the same process that didn't work the first time resulting in the same failure a second time. See your failures as learning experiences, which have taught you what not to do, and do it differently. If you are not sure how, go to the neighbour whose greenhouse is blossoming in abundance and ask him how he did it.

Parents are the first to place a seed in their children's minds. I have seen toddlers with bigger dreams than most. They want to be

Superman, or a glowing princess fairy. There are no obstacles in their minds at this young age and they dream about being the greatest. They dress up and play the role, truly believing that they are this wonderful character. In their role play they are at the very top. When playing shop, the little girl or boy owns the shop. When playing house, the little girl or boy is the head chef of the kitchen. In all cases the child is the boss. Their attitude in this role will depend on the influence and teaching they have received in their own home. It is fun to watch them. I hear their words and instructions, just the way their parents would say it to them. Children put all their trust in their parents and believe everything they tell them. They are little sponges and will repeat all they hear and see, so we do our best to create a positive and loving home for them to grow. Families are perfectly made up of imperfect people whom we love and respect just they way they are. It is a shame that we cannot choose their first schoolteacher, who has the huge responsibility of allowing each child to progress the seeds that we first planted in their thoughts. We throw them into a classroom, with tens of others, an array of personalities, all led by a stranger. Then they are taught a bunch of rules and regulations, but most of all they are taught limitations. In many cases they are taught that they are not good enough if they are not as fast or as academically smart as the next kid. Teachers expect each child to learn at the same pace and level as each other, and if they don't, they label that child as weak, or misbehaved. This trend has a negative impact on the little boy who is a genius on his computer, and on the little girl who is a genius at designing. They are expected to focus on their weakness instead of their strengths. The dyslexic child is told to learn off poetry and gets reprimanded when they simply cannot rhyme if all off the same as a non-dyslexic child. When it comes to sports, the school conducts fitness tests on the child and those with shorter legs and less stamina are labelled as unfit when they don't reach the expected number on the fitness table. Who decided that everyone should be at the same levels? Who decided that there is a number on a chart for all the children to run at the same speed within the same timeframe? This is a sure way to destroy confidence and a child's self-worth.

Life lessons including nutrition, survival skills, and positivity should be on the school syllabus. They should include lessons on equality and inequality and knowing the difference. Children should be encouraged to work on their strengths. They should never be labelled or segregated or categorized according to their abilities. Each one of them has a unique talent, and sometimes it takes them longer than others to discover theirs. Early school days should be used to introduce them to all the different subjects and allow them to explore and trial all this new knowledge at their own pace. No grading, and no labelling, so that they all learn to respect each other, just the way they are. These are years of discovery. These are the years that will determine how they progress in school for the more difficult years to come. Children are innocent little persons, beginning the journey of life. They are not perfect. When you seek perfection in others, especially in your children you will be undoubtedly disappointed.

We must support and encourage and love them unconditionally. Remember, childhood is the preparation for adulthood, so these early years are the most important.

Whenever I attend an event, whether it's a local play with the kids, or a big sporting event, the sign says €5 for OAP's and children and €10 for all those in between. I never understood the logic in this. The OAP's have lived longer so they should have more than all the rest. Did they really blow all their life savings? I doubt it. If they had saved only €5 a week for 50 years, they would have a nice little stash built up, not to mention all the assets they have built up over the years. Don't be fooled by the fairy-tale of the little old lady or the little old man. They have so much more knowledge and experience. They have worked hard over the years and should now be enjoying the fruits of their labour. I welcome the wisdom that comes with getting older because my life is a gift and I appreciate all that I have. It is sad that the new generation don't listen to us older folks. I heard a quote one time that History is just a repeat of mankind making the same mistakes over again, because they didn't learn from the previous generations. This is so true. They don't want to hear our advice. They say that they're situation is different, so they go ahead and make the same mistakes that we did. Imagine if each generation did actually listen and learn from the previous one. The world would increase in prosperity and peace year after year. Each generation would continue to add knowledge, wisdom, and solutions to make the world a happier and more peaceful place to live.

'I am grateful to be old, because many of my good friends and family never got the pleasure'

Chapter 8

My Later Years

In my late fifties I was diagnosed with diabetes type 2. I knew little to nothing about the condition, and when I asked my doctor what the outcome would be, he answered 'It just means that you will age much faster', and there is no cure. He gave me some medication and signed me up to attend the Diabetic Clinic once a month in the hospital. When I left the doctor, I thought about what he had said. For a short while, I dwelt on his words, which left me apprehensive. I wasn't an old man, and I had no intentions of becoming a typical old man. In my mind, I pictured someone sitting in a rocking chair with a walking stick by his side, so I wasn't too thrilled about the idea. I had lived a heathy life, with no sickness or serious hospital admissions to date. I had always been physically strong in every respect, so this news came as an unwelcome blow. However, I continued to work as normal, but over time, it began to have an impact on my health and wellbeing. When I attended the diabetic clinic, I met with others in the same position, who complained about their condition. Some of them talked about their kidneys failing, others about their eyesight deteriorating significantly, and some even talked about getting their leg amputated. I left the clinic that day feeling deflated and dreaded the days ahead. I followed the diet plan that the diabetic nutritionist prescribed, but nothing seemed to alleviate the symptoms. My blood sugar levels just wouldn't come back to near normal, and it was frustrating.

I heard of many deaths including some of my friends, who had also long suffered with the condition. I went through minor surgical procedures, and for a time trips to different hospitals throughout the country were numerous and I dreaded what more was to come.

One afternoon, while I sat having some lunch, I had a conversation with a friend whom I told that this thing was beating me. He said he had known me to be an undefeated person of great positivity and determination, and one who didn't easily give up on anything. This being true, I decided to delve into some research, and see if there was anything more that I could do to save myself. To my amazement, my research, with the help of others, unveiled a new light. It dawned on me that the people at the clinic, the nutritionists, and some of the doctors, were all doing the same thing for the same people for years, which was leading them to death's door. I had always told myself that if something is not working, don't keep doing it – try a different path. And here I was following the instructions of those who weren't succeeding. I began to watch stories and listen to the people who were diagnosed with Diabetes like me, and who had managed to reverse it. I was amazed. Nobody had told me that this was possible. These are the people I needed to follow. With the help of a faithful friend, a new diet and exercise plan was created, and I began a new lifestyle. I followed the plan to the letter and made sure that I reached my goal of walking ten thousand steps every day. Several weeks went passed and I was enjoying the new change. I looked forward to my walk in the evenings. I took the time, no matter the weather, to enjoy the fresh air and the ambience of that time alone. After about twelve weeks,

I lost two stone of weight, and my blood sugar levels returned to almost normal. Sometimes they even dropped to the levels of that of a person with no diabetes. During my biannual visit to the Diabetic Blood Count Clinic, the doctor said that whatever I was doing, I was doing great. I was beating it. I amazed myself. The condition was still there, but I was out of danger. I had it under control. Had I researched some years earlier, I may have been able to reverse it completely. However, I was a new man, looking and feeling better than ever. I threw away the pills. Every pill I had taken, was causing an adverse effect on something else. One pill led to needing another pill, and that pill caused another problem. Every pill that helped something, created something else that needed fixing. I was finished with them all. I continued to learn about new foods and their affects, and I was very self-disciplined. I even bought some of the same bean and pea shoots that Aunt Susan used to eat from her garden and thought of how she enjoyed a long disease-free life. I was also able to enjoy treats here and there, without feeling guilty. Many in the world around me continued to suffer, and I wanted to share this good news with them. When you put your positive mindset to work, and never give up, there is always a way. Sometimes we need to stop feeling sorry for ourselves, stop complaining, and believe in yourself. When I look back and think of when I was first diagnosed, I was led to believe that there was no way out. I was surrounded by negative situations, presenting doom and gloom. I allowed myself to be part of this for a time, which had an adverse effect on my thoughts. It is so important to remember that our environment impacts our thoughts, which develops our mindset. Our mindset decides our actions in every situation. Now, the trips to the diabetic clinic were no longer negative. For me they became just an appointment to confirm that I was doing just great. I smiled at the others who waited in line, but never allowed their sad stories to take hold of my thoughts. Whenever I was asked how I was doing, I said 'Great'. When some asked how is your diabetes, I would say 'What diabetes? I don't have diabetes'.

'Never give up on yourself'

I thought of one of my favourite stories I had heard about reaching for something you thought was impossible to achieve. There was a young boy walking through a field. He saw a herd of cattle, but being a farmer's son, he was used to them and continued his walk. However, as he got closer, he saw the huge bull peering out from behind the cattle. This was not good. The bull began rolling his foot in the grass, getting ready to charge. The young boy had only seconds to think. He glanced around the field, and knowing he didn't have long, and that he would never reach the gate on time, he ran towards a tree with an overhanging branch in the distance. He could feel the vibration of the hoofs of the bull charging after him. When he approached the tree, and knowing he had only one chance, he jumped as high as he could, but missed the branch. However, he caught it on the way down. You see, this was life or death. He reached beyond his ability and amazed himself by his ability to reach higher than his own expectations.

Did you know that the meaning of Luck is success brought by chance, rather than by one's own actions? Therefore, I never believed in saying Good Luck to someone. Good luck is for success through taking a bet, whether on the lottery or a draw. These are little gimmicks in life that provide entertainment. Sometimes you win and
sometimes you lose. We have no control over the results. Don't go through life wishing good luck on yourself, rely only on your own honest work, for winning and reaping what you sow. My three main priorities in life are in the order

of God first, Family second, and my work third. They don't always appear in this order though. I remember a very posh lady, upstanding and well thought of within the community. She dressed smartly and was always involved in Church roles and events. She would walk down the isle of the church with her hands joined together in an almost saintly pose. She rhymed off all the prayers and sang all the hymns. One morning on her way to Church, she passed by an elderly gentleman, who walked to Church every morning. She waved to him, as she watched him trip and fall against a stone wall. He lay there, his leg bleeding and he reached his hand out to her. The lady didn't want to be late for Church, so she ignored his call for help and continued driving past. She left the man there in pain to bleed. She certainly didn't have her priorities straight that day. I wondered if God appreciated her solemn prayers and hymns that morning. As far as I was concerned, she, like many others with joined hands, were there for appearance. They lacked the wisdom to understand the true meaning of life and passed by opportunities to show compassion for mankind. What good are the prayers? What good are the appearances?

'Don't count the things you do, Do the things that count'

Life in this world is short. The world as I know it since I was born in 1943, has changed and expanded beyond our expectations. New inventions, easy travel and technology have changed the world we live in. As a kid, the furthest I travelled was 14 miles into the nearest town, which took 4 hours on the horse and cart. Now, I can be in New York in 6 hours. Progression is great and I embrace it, but it comes with a downside too. My family had no debts, no mortgages and no connection with banks or loan sharks. We had no electric or phone bills. Life was simpler and we lived within our means. When I see a young couple starting out in married life together today, they start in debt. They are building huge 4- and 5-bedroom homes, filled with expensive furniture and gardens with sheds, car ports and playgrounds. The bigger and more elaborate the better. Then they both must work to pay for it. They will spend the next 25 to 30 years working to pay for a house which they can only enjoy on their rare days off. They will each need a car which they will buy on finance, so it's not really their own. Then they get another loan to take a holiday once a year. Then there are the electricity bills, and the phone and internet bills. They spend their lives working for banks and finance companies, rather than for themselves. When the weekend comes, there is very little left in the kitty for themselves to enjoy. Even though their wealth has increased, they have created debts and bills beyond their means. It's no wonder that stress has become the biggest killer in the world. The rates of separations, divorces, depression, and suicides have increased. Is this really a better way of life? With all the progression, they are no better off than before. Live within your means. Less is always best and choose to live for enjoyment and fulfilment, putting your family first. A small car will get you from A to B, the same as a big car. You can buy a big house, but you cannot buy a happy home. Base your priorities on what really matters because material things are temporary and unnecessary. They don't create happiness, only debt, which creates unhappiness.

When I look back on my life, I am pleased with my achievements. I am enjoying these years the same as I enjoyed my younger years. I may not be as physically able, but I haven't changed otherwise. On the journey of life, we have several different stages, and each stage puts us in different positions. There is a time to laugh, a time to cry, a time to celebrate, and a time mourn. There is a time to fall and a time to rise. There is also a time to be quiet and a time to talk.

Last year, in the depths of the winter snow, I foolishly walked to the top of a steep graveyard to meet a customer who wanted to purchase a family tombstone. The snow lay on top of a layer of ice, so it was difficult to manoeuvre between the stones and the hidden grass. After a few minutes of chatting, I got out my measuring tape and took a long step to the right. My foot slid from under me, and I could feel my body giving way. I fell to the ground, my hip being the first to smack down onto the iced covered concrete path. I couldn't breathe. When I eventually got home, I dragged my body over the driveway to reach the front door of the house. My family helped me to bed and arranged a trip to the hospital. After some x-rays, it was confirmed that I had shattered the ball bone in my hip socket. I was devastated. Because of the awkward area of the injury, a cast was out of the question. In a split second, I had become disabled. My life had stopped. I couldn't walk. Every time I moved; I could feel excruciating pain. The simple everyday tasks like going to the bathroom or sitting up to grab something became unbearable. I was confined to my bed for three months. I could barely sit up to look out through the window and I was in agony. It was during the COVID 19 pandemic, so the hospital and physio visits were daunting tasks with the addition of mask wearing, vaccines and paperwork. The most devasting part of this event in my life, was the inability to anything. I could suffer the pain, but I couldn't suffer the confinement. I missed driving my car, going to work, going for my evening walks, and the freedom that I had previously taken for granted. I thought about my factory every day, but after a while I stopped worrying because I had no choice but to leave it in the hands of my employees. With a positive mindset, I decided to not dwell on the things I couldn't do and focus on the things that I could do. It was a time of great thought and remembrance of days passed. I began to think of all the things I had achieved in my life, and about all the people I had met along the way. I thought about my family and all the places I had travelled to. All of my thoughts inspired me to write this book. I wanted to share my life story and my experiences. It would pass the time and bring me back to the happiest times in my life. I cast my mind back to my childhood days and laughed to myself at the antics fun we had growing up. I remembered all the people who were with me on my journey and those who were against me, which I also laughed at. I gathered all my memories and jotted them down and set a new goal to write this book.

Positively moving forward, after three long months, I walked for the first time. I didn't care that I hobbled awkwardly on one leg. I didn't care that it hurt every time I put one foot in front of the other. I was able to walk and had a little private celebration party in my mind. I gave much consideration to others in the same situation as myself, particularly to those who had no hope of recovering. As for me, it was only a matter of time until I was out and about again, and I felt blessed that this was the case. I couldn't imagine living out the rest of my days without my independence. I was back on the road. It felt like I was driving for the first time all over again, and I was elated. I laughed at myself, being so joyous at this age, for achieving the simple goals of a child. I was good at laughing at myself. I always preferred to laugh than

to worry especially at things over which I had no control. I am back at work, although not as involved in the day to day running of the factory. I am not sure if my leg will ever completely recover, as I am still hobbling along on my way. The long walks are a distant memory, but apart from walking and taking part in marathons, there is nothing that I cannot do. I have many more years ahead of me and I am looking forward to what they will bring.

Chapter 9

My Favourite Quotes and Affitmations

Some of my favourite positive affirmations and quotes from successful people around the world:

- You don't have to be a winner to start, but you have to be a winner to get started.

- The 11th commandment: Thou shall not kid thyself

- If you go out looking for a friend, they are very scarce, but if you go out to be a friend, they are everywhere.

- There are no traffic jams on the extra mile

- Some people find fault as if there were a reward for it

- Don't be distracted by criticism. The only taste of success they have is when they take a bite out of you.

- When you see a person without a smile, give them one of yours.

- People say that money is the route of all evil, but I say that the lack of money is the root of all evil.

- It's a quiet and peaceful place at the top because there are not many there.

- Always do the right things for your brand.

- Your business is the people first. Help them to help yourself.

- Don't compare yourself with anyone else, or you will insult yourself.

- If you think you can do a thing, or you can't do a thing, you're right.

- Failure is the chance to do it again, more intelligently.

- You can't build a reputation on what you are going to do

- Obstacles are those frightful things you see when you take your mind off your goal.

- Employers only handle the money, it's the customer that pays the wages.

- Nothing is hard if you divide into small tasks.

- A man cannot leave his business – he

must think of it by day and dream of it by night.

- There is no happiness except in the joy that we have accomplished something.

- If you don't like something change it, if you can't, change your attitude.

- Someone is sitting in the shade today because someone planted a tree a long time ago.

- My actions take me closer to my greater purpose.

- I was not created to imitate someone else.

- My mood doesn't depend on other people's opinions.

- I cannot change someone else, but I can choose to stay positive

Afterward

This has been a short book on personal memories of mine. I have lived a long, prosperous life, and I wish to leave on my legacy and wisdom for anyone who wishes to take the same path. Remember: the confidence and drive are inside you. Don't let anyone tell you otherwise. Seek the necessary resources, listen, and learn from the masters of the craft, take a step forward, and take control of your life. Don't be the falling leaf in the wind. Be the strong and proud mountain that with stands all storms. I wish everyone reading this a step forward in their lives and careers. No matter how small, progress is progress. Do not be afraid to take that leap of faith. Trust yourself, and onward you go.

Acknowledgements

This book is the essence of decades spent in this world, with sweat, tears and elbow grease that has gone through the experiences that have made this journey worthwhile. I wish to thank every person I ever befriended, every kind word spoken to me, every book I read, and every sunrise that shone on my soul and path.